PICTURE HISTORY OF GERMAN AND DUTCH PASSENGER SHIPS

William H. Miller, Jr.

Dover Publications, Inc.
Mineola, New York

This book is dedicated to

DER SCUTT

*Brilliant Architect, Master Ship Collector
and Supportive Friend*

Copyright

Copyright © 2002 by William H. Miller, Jr.
All rights reserved under Pan American and International Copyright Conventions.

Published in the United Kingdom by David & Charles, Brunel House, Forde Close, Newton Abbot, Devon TQ12 4PU.

Bibliographical Note

Picture History of German and Dutch Passenger Ships is a new work, published by Dover Publications, Inc., in 2002.

Library of Congress Cataloging-in-Publication Data

Miller, William H., 1948–
    Picture history of German and Dutch passenger ships / William H. Miller, Jr.
      p. cm.
    ISBN 0-486-42063-9 (pbk.)
    1. Ocean liners—Germany—History—20th century—Pictorial works. 2. Ocean liners—Netherlands—History—20th century—Pictorial works. I. Title.
VM381 .M449826 2002
387.2'432'0943—dc21

2002017413

Book design by Carol Belanger Grafton

Manufactured in the United States of America
Dover Publications, Inc., 31 East 2nd Street, Mineola, N.Y. 11501

Contents

ACKNOWLEDGMENTS / vi

FOREWORD *by Arnold Kludas* / vii

PHOTO CREDITS / viii

INTRODUCTION / ix

CHAPTER 1
The 1920s: Revival and Renewal / 1

CHAPTER 2
The 1930s: Economics, Politics and the Eve of War / 22

CHAPTER 3
The 1940s: War, Destruction and Decline / 63

CHAPTER 4
The 1950s: Rebirth and Rebuilding / 70

CHAPTER 5
The 1960s: A Shift in Trades / 95

CHAPTER 6
The Modern Age of Cruising / 100

BIBLIOGRAPHY / 116

INDEX OF SHIPS / 117

Acknowledgments

Creating a book like this takes many hands. I am merely the general organizer, the arranger, the catalyst. After determining the basic chronology, I reach out for the prized photographs. Very few come from my own files. Some are in private hands; some are nearby, others far off. There are always a few that are especially difficult to find or to borrow. In the case of this book, the superb archives of Hapag-Lloyd in Hamburg have been invaluable. In particular, Hans-Jurgen Capell has been a wonderful assistant and most generous friend. Arnold Kludas has been equally important, providing not only rare photos but prized anecdotes and insights, as well as the fine honor of his foreword. He has always been a great inspiration to me, and an enormous source of information and reference. His many books are among the greatest ocean liner guides ever published.

As always, of course, I am especially grateful to Dover Publications for designing, producing, and publishing so expertly these photographic studies of the great passenger ships. I shall always be particularly thankful to the late Hayward Cirker, founder and president of Dover, who assisted and encouraged me. Highest praises to the excellent editorial staff at Dover, in particular to Drew Silver, who meticulously edited the text and the captions, and to Irene Kupferman, conscientious and professional typesetter; and to Carol Grafton, whose designs for this and previous ocean liner books have contributed so much to their success.

Richard Faber is another superb friend and extraordinary source of information and photographs. Most generous and ever patient, he has been a great help with this book in particular. Great thanks also to other dear and supportive friends: Ernest Arroyo, Frank Braynard, Tom Cassidy, Anthony Cooke, the late Frank Cronican, the late John Gillespie, Hisashi Noma, Richard Morse, Der Scutt, Gordon Turner, and the late Everett Viez. And my greatest appreciation to Abe Michaelson, my business partner, who assists greatly by dispatching copies of these maritime books to just about every corner of the earth. He is an indispensable link to the world.

Others due thanks include Philippe Brebant, Stephen Card, Michael Cassar, Luis Miguel Correia, Alex Duncan, Laurence Dunn, Maurizio Eliseo, Andres Hernandez, Hans Hoffmann, David Hutchings, Peter Knego, Jan Loeff, Victor Marinelli, Mitchell Mart, Rolf Meinecke, Peter Newall, Ove Nielsen, Robert Pabst, Paolo Piccione, Frank Pichardo, Fred Rodriguez, Selim San, Sal Scannella, the late Roger Scozzafava, Roger Sherlock, Captain Ed Squire, Don Stoltenberg, Daniel Trachtenberg, the late Captain Cornelius van Herk, Steffen Weirauch, David Williams, and Victor Young. Organizations that have assisted include Carmania Press Limited, Crystal Cruises, Cunard Line, Fotoflite, German-Atlantic Line, Hamburg-South America Line, Holland America Line, Lloyd Werft, Mainmast Books, Nederland Line, Nedlloyd Group, the Peabody-Essex Museum, Peter Deilmann Cruises, the Port Authority of New York and New Jersey, Royal Rotterdam Lloyd, Steamship Historical Society of America, United States Coast Guard, Wilton-Fijenoord Shipyard, and the World Ship Society, especially the Port of New York branch.

Foreword

Bill Miller has been an enthusiast of passenger liners since his childhood. That is what we have in common. Bill saw his first liners in the 1950s in New York; my own first glances of these grand ships took place in the 1930s in the port of Hamburg. Our mutual interest brought us together one day at Bremerhaven in the summer of 1982, and since then we quite often meet each other—in Hamburg, Southampton, New York, or on the high seas onboard such great international cruise ships such as the *Vistafjord* and *Europa*.

When Bill asked me last year to write the foreword for this book, I agreed at once. Bill has his own special method to fascinate his readers in his many books on liners and cruise ships. In trying to explain his successful method of producing these books almost as if on a conveyor belt, one finds the following answers: on his countless cruises, Bill interviews people around the world, among them some of the last witnesses of bygone eras of passenger shipping—the passengers, staff, and managers of the present cruise industry as well as his many friends among the world's ship lovers. Further, Bill has access to photographic treasures in private and public collections all over the world. All this he puts together in his unique style of writing and organization, mixing facts and anecdotes about ships and their people, and the result is always a thrilling, very readable, and excellently illustrated book.

Bill Miller's series of beautiful books on the efforts of each nation to build and maintain passenger liners is an impressive and worthy monument to these great ships.

ARNOLD KLUDAS
Grunendeich, Germany
June 2001

Arnold Kludas is Germany's foremost maritime historian and author. He has written over 40 books on all aspects of shipping, with his works on passenger liners being especially noteworthy.

Photo Credits

Frank O. Braynard Collection: 3 (top), 46 (top)
Michael Cassar: 108 (top), 113 (bottom)
Luis Miguel Correia Collection: 58 (top), 106 (bottom), 107 (top), 109, 110 (top), 110 (bottom)
Cronican-Arroyo Collection: 4, 7, 8 (top), 8 (center), 9, 10, 21 (top), 24 (top), 27 (top), 27 (center), 27 (bottom), 29 (bottom), 30 (left), 30–31, 32, 40–41, 47, 48 (bottom), 50, 51 (top), 53, 55 (bottom), 60 (top), 64 (top), 64 (bottom), 65, 66, 77, 89 (top)
Peter Dielmann Cruises: 112
Alex Duncan: 34 (top)
Richard Faber Collection: 3 (bottom), 5 (top), 5 (bottom), 6 (top), 13 (top), 13 (bottom), 14 (top), 14 (bottom), 16 (center), 16 (bottom), 18 (top), 18 (center), 18 (bottom), 20, 21 (bottom), 24 (bottom), 26 (top), 26 (center), 26 (bottom), 28 (top), 28 (bottom), 29 (top), 44 (top), 44 (bottom), 45 (top), 45 (bottom), 52, 56 (top), 56 (center), 56 (bottom), 69 (bottom), 75 (top), 75 (bottom), 76 (bottom), 79 (top), 87 (bottom), 99 (top), 99 (bottom)
German-Atlantic Line: 98 (bottom)
Gillespie-Faber Collection: ii–iii, 12, 33 (top), 38 (bottom), 59, 69 (center), 80 (top), 80 (bottom), 81, 86, 90–91, 93, 96 (bottom), 97, 98 (top)
Hamburg-South America Line: 15, 16 (top), 17
Hapag-Lloyd Archives: 6 (bottom), 8 (bottom), 19, 23 (top), 23 (bottom), 25, 39, 43 (top), 43 (bottom), 46 (bottom), 48 (top), 57, 83 (top), 84 (bottom), 85 (top), 85 (center), 85 (bottom), 89 (bottom), 96 (top), 102 (bottom), 103 (top left), 103 (top right), 113 (top)

Andres Hernandez Collection: 34 (bottom), 38 (top), 61, 62, 68
Hans Hoffmann: 114
Holland America Line: 11 (top), 11 (bottom), 49, 51 (bottom), 54, 72 (top), 72 (bottom), 73 (top), 76 (top), 78, 92 (top), 92 (center), 92 (bottom), 94, 101 (top), 103 (bottom), 104 (top), 104 (bottom), 105 (top), 105 (bottom), 107 (bottom), 115
Holland-Africa Line: 79 (bottom)
David Hutchings Collection: 37 (bottom)
Rolf Meinecke: 83 (bottom), 88
William H. Miller, Jr. Collection: 101 (bottom), 111
Moran Towing & Transportation Company: 106 (top)
Richard K. Morse Collection: 82
Nederland Line: 35, 36
Ove Nielsen: 108 (bottom)
Robert Pabst: 60 (bottom)
Peabody Essex Museum: 2
Port Authority of New York and New Jersey: 71
Rotterdam Lloyd: 33 (center), 33 (bottom)
Royal Rotterdam Lloyd: 38 (center), 67 (top), 67 (bottom)
Selim San: 73 (bottom)
Roger Scozzafava: 74
Roger Sherlock: 42, 87 (top)
Skyfotos International: 37 (top)
Gordon Turner Collection: 84 (top)
U.S. Coast Guard: 102 (top)
Cornelius van Herk Collection: 58 (bottom)
Steffen Weirauch Collection: 69 (top), 99 (center)
Wilton-Fijenoord Shipyard: 55 (top)

Introduction

This book continues a series begun years ago, of single-volume photo histories of French, Italian, American and, most recently, British liners, all published by Dover. For this book, however, I decided to combine the Dutch and German liner fleets, and begin coverage just after the First World War.

After the war, the Dutch fleet was largely intact and carrying on its unglamorous but solid trade on the North Atlantic run, to the East and the West Indian colonies, and to South America, Africa and the Far East. The German lines, on the other hand, had lost almost all of what, before 1914, had been one of the world's largest and most important passenger ship fleets. Among other ships, they had lost the three largest liners yet built (the *Imperator*, the *Vaterland*, and the *Bismarck*), taken by the Allies at the war's end (becoming the *Berengaria*, the *Leviathan*, and the *Majestic*, respectively). They lost all but one of their great four-stackers as well as the likes of the *George Washington*, the *Tirpitz*, and the first *Columbus* (which went on to become the British *Homeric* [not to be confused with the one shown in this book]). By 1919, the German passenger fleet was all but completely stripped. Rebuilding in the 1920s was a major undertaking, requiring a major financial commitment.

Within a decade—by the time of the Wall Street Crash of 1929—the German fleet had been triumphantly revived. The *Cap Arcona*, completed in 1927, for example, was not only the largest and fastest, but most luxurious liner on the South Atlantic, sailing from Hamburg to ports along the east coast of South America. Two years later, beginning in the summer of 1929, the recently-defeated nation produced not one but two of the fastest superliners ever to sail the North Atlantic—the mighty near-sisters *Bremen* and *Europa*. Stunning the British shipping industry, they took the prized Blue Ribbon away from Cunard's veteran *Mauretania*.

The Dutch fleet advanced as well, with such new liners as the *Statendam*, the largest Dutch liner yet on the run to New York, and with two sets of sister ships, the *Johan van Oldenbarnevelt* and *Marnix van St. Aldegonde*, and the *Baloeran* and *Dempo*, the biggest and the finest ships to date on the East Indian colonial routes. The lean Depression years of the 1930s also produced such ships as the *Nieuw Amsterdam*, the *Oranje*, and *Patria*.

The Second World War again devastated the German liner fleet and took a toll on the Dutch as well. By late 1945, the entire German fleet was gone: sunk, damaged, or taken by the victorious Allies. Under strict postwar restrictions, companies such as North German Lloyd were not even permitted to restore their Atlantic passenger service for a full ten years, until 1955. Meanwhile, the Dutch rebuilt slowly, adding ships such as the *Willem Ruys*, the *Tjiwangi*, and the sisters *Maasdam* and *Ryndam*.

By 1959, following a decade-long boom in liner travel, the Dutch fleet was headed by a brand new *Rotterdam* and the West German by an extensively rebuilt *Bremen*. Their success hinted at a promising future for traditional, class-divided transocean passenger shipping. But in fact, time was running short. By the mid-1960s, the airlines, newly equipped with speedy jet aircraft, lured away even the most loyal of ocean voyagers. Soon, of necessity, the whole purpose of the passenger ship business changed. As the older liners lost their trade and faded away, a new era began: the age of the full-time, all-first-class cruise ship. Hapag-Lloyd (created by the merger of the Hamburg America and North German Lloyd lines) and Holland America were among those companies that accepted this as their future. Soon, they would build purposely-designed vacation ships—sleek, amenity-filled floating resorts with luxurious lounges and large cabins, casinos and health centers, pool-fitted lido decks and shopping arcades.

By the late 1990s, as I began my notes for this book, both the Dutch and German cruise fleets were still expanding. Holland America, for example, had ordered its largest liners yet, a pair of 84,000-tonners, while the Germans had commissioned the *Deutschland*, said to be one of the most luxurious liners ever to put to sea.

In April 2000, I visited the maritime museums in Rotterdam and Amsterdam. I was inspired by their vast collections of models, artifacts, paintings, and photos. A few months later in Hamburg, I visited Arnold Kludas, undoubtedly Germany's greatest maritime historian. He encouraged me to do this book, shared some rare photos and kindly agreed to write the foreword. "There is great history in ocean liners—their ingenuity, their innovation, their creation, and even in their destruction," he said. "There can never be enough photos, facts, anecdotes." These visits cemented my plan for this book. I have followed Arnold's suggestion and with this book, I hope, added something to the story of Dutch and German passenger ships.

BILL MILLER
Secaucus, New Jersey
November 2001

CHAPTER ONE

The 1920s: Revival and Renewal

The Museum of Maritime Industry is located in New York City, just a few miles from the once bustling piers of Manhattan, at the New York State Maritime College at Fort Schuyler in the Bronx. While largely a testament to American ships and shipowners, and to New York harbor itself, it contains a number of display models representing foreign ships. These extraordinary replicas are big, detailed, and extremely valuable in today's marine collectible market. They are almost irreplaceable today. The cost alone would be staggering. There are brass lifeboat davits, for example, intricate rigging and even real pieces of canvas over the lifeboats and as awnings. Three of them, ten to fifteen feet in length, reproduce ships discussed in this book. There is the *Albert Ballin* and the *Reliance* of the Hamburg America Line and, biggest of all, the *Bremen*, the great record-breaker of 1929, which sailed for North German Lloyd. The full-hull model of the *Bremen* with her original squat funnels and the airplane and catapult between them was recently said to be worth $250,000. North German Lloyd, the original owner, wanted it returned and offered the museum up to five other models, all of freighters and container ships, in trade. The museum politely declined. Like the two other German liner models, this replica of the *Bremen* came to the museum in 1939–40, when the German shipping companies closed their American offices at the start of the Second World War. The models were sent to Fort Schuyler for safekeeping and have never left.

The *Albert Ballin*, the *Reliance*, and the *Bremen* were creations of the 1920s. Following the devastation of the First World War, the resumption of luxury passenger service represented a new beginning, a revival, not only for the ships' owners, but for Germany. The reconstruction was extraordinary. North German Lloyd, for example, a company that had had a large fleet before the war, including some of the world's largest, fastest, and grandest liners, ended it with a single ship, the 800-ton freighter *Grussgott*. By 1929, it had over 50. That year, it introduced the new *Bremen*, which was not only one of the world's largest and most luxurious ocean liners, but the fastest ship of any kind then afloat. The company was rightfully proud.

The 1920s were a period of rebuilding. The principal German shipping companies had been almost entirely stripped, and the Dutch had to replace many ships lost during the War. In the early 20s the lines were moderate and cautious in their approach. They planned conservatively, not for huge or splendid or even very fast ships, but quite modest ones. One important consideration was that the US government had begun to reduce drastically the flow of immigrants onto its shores. On the Atlantic run to New York, for example, 1.4 million had crossed in the year before the war started; by 1924, the total was just 150,000. Clearly, the brisk, quick profits to be made from steerage and third-class passengers were gone. Improved lower-deck quarters, some renamed "tourist class," were now the order of the day.

By the late twenties, however, cautious conservatism gave way to a surge of new, bigger expectations. North German Lloyd, for example, had been planning two 35,000-ton near-sisters to its highly successful *Columbus* of 1924. These soon evolved into a pair of 40,000-tonners and then to record-breaking 50,000-ton ships. They became the extraordinary *Bremen* and *Europa* of 1929–30. Another German shipowner, the Hamburg-South America Line, added the 27,000-ton *Cap Arcona*, often said to be one of the finest ships on the Europe-South America run. Similarly, Holland America introduced its largest ship to date, the 29,500-ton *Statendam*, in 1929. For German and Dutch passenger ship owners, the twenties were busy times.

HANSA ⤳ Germany produced some of the world's largest, fastest and most luxurious "floating palaces" in the fifteen or so years before the First World War. No fewer than five four-stackers snatched records from British ships. Biggest and perhaps most overwhelming of all were the successively larger near-sisters built to dominate the Atlantic run: the *Imperator* (1913), the *Vaterland* (1914), and the *Bismarck* (not yet completed at the start of the war). The biggest ships the world had yet seen, by 1919 they were either gone—lost in combat or seized by the Allies in overseas ports—or about to be taken as reparations. Three of the four-stackers, for example, were in American hands, as were the *George Washington*, the *Amerika*, and the *Vaterland*, which had been acquired by the Navy and rechristened USS *Leviathan* in 1917 (it later became the United States Lines' *Leviathan*). The *Imperator* went to the British as Cunard's *Berengaria*, and the *Bismarck* was ordered completed at Hamburg for the White Star Line and renamed *Majestic*. It was the largest liner afloat and was immensely prestigious and popular.

The Germans were left with only one large ship, Hamburg America's former *Deutschland*. When completed in 1900, she had captured the transatlantic Blue Ribbon for speed, crossing at nearly 22.5 knots. She had considerable problems, however: noisy engines; excessive vibration; on one occasion she even lost her rudder and stern post. By 1910–11, she was pulled off the Atlantic express run and refitted as cruise ship. Renamed *Victoria Luise*, her four-class capacity of 2,050 was reduced to 487, all first class. During the war, there were plans to make her an armed auxiliary cruiser, but her mechanical problems were too serious. She sat out the war years unused, rusting and in deepening decay, and was the one large ship rejected by the Allies in 1918–19. She was refitted by Hamburg America as an (outmoded) immigrant carrier, the *Hansa* (**above**). Her once impressive four funnels were replaced by two, and her return to service was delayed by at least two fires during conversion in October and November 1920. She was used in Hamburg–New York and later Hamburg–Halifax service (she is seen here leaving Pier 86 in New York). Germany's first big liner of the 1920s, she was scrapped in 1925 at Hamburg. [Built by Vulkan Shipyards, Stettin, Germany, 1900. 16,333 gross tons; 684 feet long; 67 feet wide. Quadruple expansion engines, twin screw. Service speed reduced to 15 knots by 1921. 1,386 passengers in 1921 (36 first-class, 1,350 third-class).]

ALBERT BALLIN / HANSA ⤳ In 1923, Hamburg America Line launched its first new postwar ship, the *Albert Ballin*, named for the company's prewar director. She and her sister, the *Deutschland*, were actually passenger-cargo ships, carrying up to 1,551 passengers and six holds of freight. Two slightly different sisters, the *Hamburg* and the *New York*, followed in 1926. They made weekly sailings between Hamburg and New York via Southampton and Cherbourg. To improve their service, they were re-engined in 1929–30 and lengthened in 1933–34.

Under pressure from the Nazi government in 1935, the *Albert Ballin* was renamed *Hansa* (Albert Ballin was Jewish). The ship is seen here (**opposite, top**) in icy waters at New York, berthed at Pier 86 in February 1938. Largely unused during World War II, she became a training ship for the German Navy in 1945, but was mined off Warnemunde on March 6. Salvaged by the Soviets in 1949, she was extensively rebuilt before re-emerging as the *Sovetsky Sojus*, the largest passenger ship under the Soviet flag, in 1955. She sailed mainly in the Far East out of Vladivostock. Renamed *Soyuz* in 1980, she was scrapped a year later. [Built by Blohm & Voss Shipbuilders, Hamburg, Germany, 1923. 20,815 gross tons as built; 627 feet long; 72 feet wide. Steam turbines, twin screw. Service speed 15.5 knots. 1,551 passengers (251 first-class, 340 second-class, 960 third-class).]

Noted for their fine food, impeccable service and unmatched cleanliness, the *Albert Ballin* (**opposite, bottom**) and her sisters were very popular. Here we see New Year's Eve celebrations on December 31, 1930.

2 / THE 1920s: REVIVAL AND RENEWAL

THE 1920s: REVIVAL AND RENEWAL / 3

HAMBURG (1926) ~ The *Hamburg* and her sister ship, the *New York*, were generally similar to the earlier *Albert Ballin* and *Deutschland*, but most noticeably differed in having only two masts instead of the four on the previous pair. Seen here docking at New York's Pier 84, at the foot of West 44th Street, in June 1935, with North German Lloyd's *Europa* to the left, the *Hamburg* (*above*) became a naval accommodation ship for the Nazis in 1940. Later, on March 7, 1945, during the evacuation of forces from the Eastern Front, she struck a mine and sank. Salvaged by the Soviets in 1950, she was restored slowly. Intended to be a passenger ship, the *Yuri Dolgoruki*, she was finished instead in 1960 as a whaling mother ship. She was broken up in 1977. [Built by Blohm & Voss Shipbuilders, Hamburg, Germany, 1926. 21,132 gross tons; 635 feet long; 72 feet wide. Steam turbines, twin screw. Service speed 15.5 knots. 1,149 passengers (222 first-class, 471 second-class, 456 third-class).]

RELIANCE ~ The histories of some German passenger ships become somewhat confusing during the 1920s. For example, the Hamburg America Line ordered several smaller versions of their huge, 52–56,000-ton *Imperator* class ships just before the First World War. (Author Noel Bonsor calls them "pocket *Imperators*.") Two of these were the sisters *William O'Swald* and *Johann Heinrich Burchard*, splendid ships intended for the run from Hamburg to ports along the east coast of South America: Rio de Janeiro, Santos (Sao Paulo), Montevideo, and Buenos Aires. (A third, very close sister was the *Admiral von Tirpitz*, later *Tirpitz*, completed in 1920; it sailed as the *Empress of Australia* for Canadian Pacific.) But construction of the first two was slowed and then halted during the war, and in 1916, they were sold to the Dutch line Royal Holland Lloyd. They were completed in 1920 as the *Brabantia* and *Limburgia* respectively, and sailed from Amsterdam to the same South American ports. But they were unsuccessful and in 1922 were sold to the United American Line, renamed *Resolute* and *Reliance*, seen here (*opposite, top*) docking at Copenhagen during a summer cruise, and put into transatlantic service between New York and Hamburg. Soon their sailings were coordinated with those of their revived former owner, Hamburg America. In 1923, because of Prohibition in the United States, the two ships were reflagged in Panama and became two of the first ships to fly a "flag of convenience." In 1926, they were sold outright to Hamburg America and for a time became two of the world's most celebrated cruise ships. The *Resolute* was sold to Italian scrappers in 1935, but was taken by the Italian government for use as a troop transport, the *Lombardia*, for Mussolini's East African campaigns. She was sunk in August 1943 during the Allied bombing of Naples and her remains were scrapped three years later. The *Reliance* burned in Hamburg harbor in August 1938 and her wreckage was scrapped in 1941. [Built by J. C. Tecklenborg Shipyard, Geestemunde, Germany, 1920. 19,582 gross tons; 615 feet long; 71 feet wide. Steam triple expansion engines, triple screw. Service speed 16 knots. 1,010 passengers (290 first-class, 320 second-class, 400 third-class).]

Both the *Reliance* (*opposite, bottom*) and the *Resolute* were noted for their splendid quarters. Here we see the entrance to the Winter Garden aboard the former. The Winter Garden, which was made to appear more spacious by the use of large mirrors, included a series of semiprivate alcoves with divans, tables, and chairs.

THE 1920s: REVIVAL AND RENEWAL / 5

6 / THE 1920S: REVIVAL AND RENEWAL

CLEVELAND ~ Another Hamburg America Line passenger ship with a varied career in the 1920s was the *Cleveland* (**opposite, top**). She and her sister, the *Cincinnati*, were fine four-masters built for both transatlantic service between Hamburg and New York and off-season cruises, including the first around-the-world tours by ship. The *Cleveland* was laid up at Hamburg for all of the First World War, and then was seized by the Americans and reconditioned as the troopship USS *Mobile* in 1919. In 1920, she was sold to the London-based Byron Steamship Company and renamed *King Alexander* for Mediterranean-New York service. She was sold again in 1923 to the United American Lines of New York, but flew Panamanian colors to avoid the restrictions of Prohibition. She reverted to the name *Cleveland* and made Atlantic crossings to and from Hamburg, a service coordinated with her original German owners. Hamburg America bought its former ship in 1926 and rehoisted the German colors. She sailed under them for another five years before being laid up, a victim of the Depression, in 1931. She was sent to the scrappers at Hamburg two years later. [Built by Blohm & Voss Shipbuilders, Hamburg, Germany, 1909. 16,960 gross tons; 607 feet long; 63 feet wide. Steam quadruple expansion engines, twin screw. Service speed 15.5 knots. 2,841 passengers as built (239 first-class, 224 second-class, 496 third-class, 1,882 steerage).]

COLUMBUS ~ Hamburg America Line's main rival, North German Lloyd, also had a slow reawakening following the First World War. In 1914 that line was building two sizeable liners for North Atlantic service, the *Columbus* and the *Hindenburg*, but construction was halted during the war years. Afterward, the intended *Columbus* was ceded to the British as reparations and later became White Star Line's *Homeric*. The second ship, renamed *Columbus* (**below**), was left in German hands in 1918, but not launched until August 1922. Completion of this ship was also rather sluggish and she did not enter service until April 1924. By far the largest liner under the German flag in the mid-1920s, she is seen here arriving at Bremerhaven, her home port, in her maiden year. [Built by Schichau Shipyards, Danzig, 1924. 32,581 gross tons; 775 feet long; 83 feet wide. Steam turbines, twin screw. Service speed 23 knots. 1,725 passengers (479 first-class, 644 tourist-class, 602 third-class).]

The first class main salon was one of the finest rooms aboard the *Columbus* (**opposite, bottom**), the flagship of North German Lloyd and Germany's finest liner, noted for her elegance, from 1924 until 1929.

The *Columbus* was nearly ruined during a summer crossing in August 1927. "The starboard shaft broke in mid-Atlantic," according to German maritime historian Arnold Kludas, "and this caused the machinery to race and nearly destroy itself." The liner was sent for repair to the Vulkan shipyard at Bremen and a substitute triple expansion engine taken from the freighter *Schwaben* was temporarily installed. Service speed was reduced for the next two years from 19 to 17.5 knots. In 1929, so that the *Columbus* might be better paired with the new, very powerful *Bremen* and *Europa*, the engine was replaced by geared turbines. Service speed increased to 22 knots, the maximum to 23 knots. The refitting also included the construction of new, squat funnels so that the *Columbus* (**top**) would appear to be a "first cousin" to the *Bremen* and *Europa*.

In this scene, dated January 3, 1938, the top sundeck of the *Columbus* (**middle**) seems a popular place. The ship herself developed a great reputation for cruising. She made short voyages to Bermuda and the Caribbean as well as extended trips around South America, Africa, and through the Mediterranean.

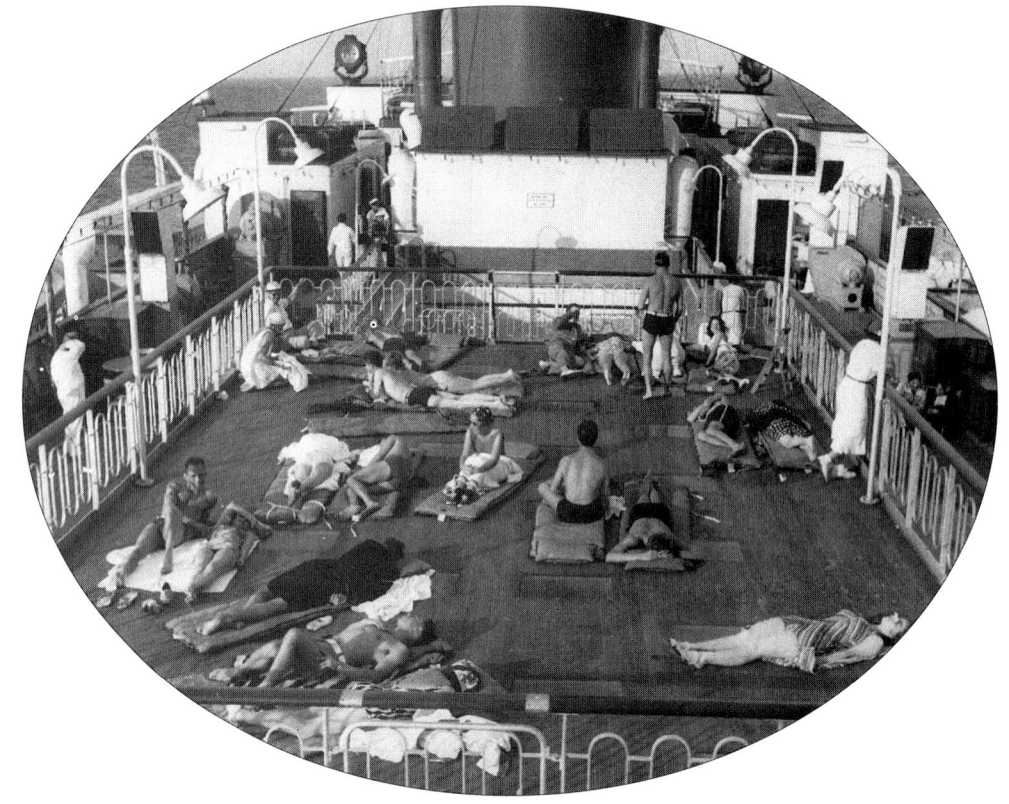

It was during a Caribbean cruise that the *Columbus* (**bottom**), seen here off Venezuela, finished her days. In August 1939, because of the imminent war in Europe, she was ordered to land her American passengers at Havana and seek sanctuary in Vera Cruz, Mexico. In December, she was summoned to Germany. Off Cape Hatteras, North Carolina, she was ordered to stop by a British destroyer, HMS *Hyperion*. Refusing to surrender the ship, the German crew set her afire and opened the sea cocks. She sank on December 19. The crew was rescued by the American cruiser USS *Tuscaloosa*.

VOLENDAM ~ The Dutch Holland America Line suffered considerable losses during the First World War. In an effort to restore its North Atlantic service between Rotterdam and New York, the company planned new passenger ship tonnage for the early 1920s. Dutch emigrants would fill the lower deck quarters, it was thought, along with a westbound surge from the Baltic states (a small steamer was acquired especially to move them to Rotterdam). Holland America turned to the noted Anglo-Irish shipbuilder Harland & Wolff and bought two ships that were on the stocks at its yard in Govan, Scotland. These had been ordered before the war, in 1914, for an intended service to Canada to be operated by a consortium of Holland America, Hamburg America, the Red Star Line, and North German Lloyd. The idea was abandoned after the war. Neither big nor fast nor especially notable in any way, they were nevertheless sturdy and comfortable. The first, the *Volendam*, had a rather difficult beginning. Her planned launching on June 23, 1922 failed when she remained stuck in the slip. Another attempt a day later also failed. Finally launched on July 6, she was later towed to Belfast for final outfitting and entered service that November. The *Veendam* followed in May 1923. Later also used for cruising, the *Volendam* (**above**) is seen here departing from her Hoboken, New Jersey berth on September 23, 1939, for a return voyage to Europe. She and her sister had mostly been evacuating worried Americans in the late summer and fall of 1939. Used as a troopship during the Second World War, she was never fully restored, but used on austerity sailings carrying immigrants, students and troops. She was broken up in 1952, her sister a year later. [Built by Harland & Wolff Limited, Govan, Scotland, 1922. 15,434 gross tons; 572 feet long; 67 feet wide. Steam turbines, twin screw. Service speed 15 knots. 1,899 passengers as built (263 first-class, 436 second-class, 1,200 third-class).]

THE 1920S: REVIVAL AND RENEWAL / 9

ROTTERDAM (1908) ~ Holland America did have a few stalwarts that survived the First World War, namely the twin-funnel *Rotterdam*, seen here *(above)* in the Kotor fjord on the Dalmatian coast during a Mediterranean cruise, and the four-master *Nieuw Amsterdam*. These continued in Atlantic service, and the *Rotterdam* did considerable cruising; she was later painted in tropical all-white and sent on a series of Caribbean trips out of New Orleans. [Built by Harland & Wolff Limited, Belfast, Ireland, 1908. 24,129 gross tons; 667 feet long; 77 feet wide. Steam quadruple expansion engines, twin screw. Service speed 17 knots. 3,575 passengers as built (520 first-class, 555 second-class, 2,500 third-class).]

The *Rotterdam*, while aging and therefore somewhat less competitive, survived the lean Depression years. Holland America, like other Dutch and German shipping companies mentioned in these pages, faced hard times, especially in the early 1930s. Following the Wall Street Crash in October 1929, over 300,000 people in the Netherlands became unemployed. Grain cargos on the Atlantic dropped by two thirds and many older ships were soon laid up. Overall passenger traffic on the Atlantic dropped from one million in 1930 to 500,000 by 1935. Holland America itself lost 7.5 million guilders in 1931, cut its staff from 3,900 to 2,600, and mandated ten percent salary cuts throughout the company. A year later, operational costs were cut by 50 percent. The veteran *Rotterdam* endured, but in 1940 age 32, went to the breakers near Rotterdam.

The *Rotterdam* had classic, quite traditional interiors. The first-class salon *(opposite, top)* included a great skylight, and first-class staterooms *(opposite, bottom)* had brass beds, rattan chairs, and bare steel ceilings. After a modernizing refit in the mid-1930s, she was advertised as the "ideal cruise ship." According to Holland America brochures, "She has a hundred and one features that appeal to vacationers. Here are just a few . . . a capacity for over 850 cruise passengers, 600 of them in outside rooms . . . modern ventilation in all rooms . . . new decorations . . . two swimming pools . . . exquisite salons . . . casino . . . Verandah Cafe . . . every corner of the ship spic and span in the true Dutch tradition of spotless cleanliness." In 1934 the *Rotterdam* offered a series of late summer and fall cruises from New York ranging from a three-and-a-half-day weekend trip to Halifax to 13 days to the Caribbean. Fares ranged from $45 to $145.

10 / THE 1920S: REVIVAL AND RENEWAL

THE 1920S: REVIVAL AND RENEWAL / 11

EDAM 〜 Soon after the war ended, in 1920 and 1921, Holland America ordered four passenger-cargo ships for service to Cuba, Mexico, and the US Gulf coast. They were the *Edam, Leerdam, Maasdam,* and *Spaarndam*. They had space for some second-class passengers and a good number of immigrants in a spartan third class. To make them seem larger and more liner-like, second, dummy funnels were added. These ships were later victims of the Depression when, in 1933–34, as their trade to the Caribbean area declined, they were downgraded for some 90 passengers each and even lost their extra funnels. After serving the Allies in the Second World War, the *Edam*, seen here (*above*) in her final years, was used on the Rotterdam-New York service, where she continued to carry passengers. She finished her days at a Hong Kong scrapyard in 1954. [Built by De Schelde shipyard, Flushing, Netherlands, 1921. 8,871 gross tons; 450 feet long; 58 feet wide. Steam turbines, single screw. Service speed 13 knots. 974 passengers as built (174 cabin-class, 800 third-class).]

STATENDAM (1929) 〜 Holland America's new flagship *Statendam*, launched by Harland & Wolff at Belfast in 1914, sat out the early years of World War I untouched. She was completed for urgent troopship duties for the British government in 1917. Renamed *Justicia*, she was to have been managed by Cunard, but went instead to the White Star Line. Her days were brief, sadly, for she was torpedoed and sunk in the North Atlantic on July 20, 1918. In 1921, the British government awarded compensation to Holland America, including a new flagship, a near-duplicate of the previous *Statendam*. Her construction time was amongst the longest for any passenger ship. Laid down in 1921, she was not launched until 1925; her incomplete hull was towed to the Netherlands in 1927 and her maiden voyage to New York did not occur until 1929. She was by then rather dated both inside and out (*opposite, top*), although always a popular, superbly served and splendidly maintained ship (she was dubbed "Queen of the Spotless Fleet"). [Built by Harland & Wolff Limited, Belfast, Northern Ireland, 1921–27; completed by Rotterdam Dry Dock Company, Rotterdam, Netherlands, 1927–29. 29,511 gross tons; 697 feet long; 81 feet wide. Steam turbines, twin screw. Service speed 19 knots. 1,654 passengers (510 first-class, 344 second-class, 426 third-class).]

In addition to her Atlantic crossings, the *Statendam* was often used as a cruise ship. She made short trips to Bermuda, Nassau and the Caribbean, as well as longer, more deluxe voyages. On February 7, 1935, for example, she left New York on a 58-day Mediterranean cruise, which took her to Madeira, Gibraltar, Cadiz, Tangier, Malaga, Algiers, Palma de Majorca, Cannes, Malta, Port Said, Haifa, Beirut, Rhodes, Istanbul, Piraeus, Corfu, Kotor, Dubrovnik, Venice, Messina, Naples, Monte Carlo, Southampton, Boulogne, and Rotterdam (where passengers could leave the ship and return on a later Holland America crossing to New York); then Boulogne, Southampton, and back to New York. Minimum fares were posted as $625 in first class, $340 in tourist class.

"Her spacious public rooms and social halls with their delightful harmony of art and craft, provide the facilities of a beautiful country club afloat," said one Holland America Line brochure of the 1930s about the *Statendam*. "In addition to the usual appointments of a modern liner, there are many special *Statendam* features, including luxurious apartments, observation palm court, gymnasium, swimming pool, Turkish bath, verandah cafe, and scientific ventilation." The handsome smoking room onboard the *Statendam* (*opposite, bottom*) was in marked contrast to the sleek, angular, Art Deco style of the 1930s, but was nevertheless a most popular shipboard space. Holland America brochures said of it: "The Smoke Room has all the attributes for masculine comfort. You will feel expansive, contented and comfortable. In the great chairs, you can sink indefinitely. And there are, of course, the games that go with a Smoking Room and a thoroughly equipped bar."

12 / THE 1920S: REVIVAL AND RENEWAL

THE 1920s: REVIVAL AND RENEWAL / 13

14 / THE 1920s: REVIVAL AND RENEWAL

Holland America Line literature often highlighted the *Statendam*'s fine cabin accommodations. "On A and B Deck, there are sixteen apartments de luxe which measure twenty-seven feet in one direction by seventeen feet in the other, and consist of a sitting room, bedroom, bathroom, and a trunk and wardrobe room. Each one has a private corridor and which gives access to the sitting room and the bathroom without the necessity of going through the bedroom. The sitting rooms in these cabins—one is shown here (*opposite, top*)—measure seventeen feet by nine; each of them has large square windows opening directly on the side of the ship, a fireplace, sofa, easy chairs, table, side chairs, and writing desk."

"The exceptionally generous pale-green swimming pool (*opposite, bottom*) is gorgeously decorated with tiles from the renowned potteries at Delft," noted a Holland America booklet. "The lighting effects give the perfect illusion of sunshine . . . a tiny bar is a happy addition. Adjoining the swimming pool is a gymnasium with the usual ambitious equipment and a Turkish bath with hot room, temperate room, cooling room and what not." Unfortunately, the beautiful *Statendam*, replaced in 1938 as the flagship of the Dutch merchant marine by the new, larger *Nieuw Amsterdam*, was a casualty of the Second World War. During the Nazi invasion of Rotterdam, on May 11, 1940, the *Statendam* was bombed, caught in a crossfire and burned out. She smoldered for five days. In August, her blistered hulk was towed to nearby Hendrik Ido Ambacht and scrapped. Some of the scrap metal later found its way to Nazi munitions factories.

CAP POLONIO ~ The passenger trade between northern Europe and the east coast of South America was a busy one in the 1920s. There were businessmen and their families, the occasional tourist and many, many emigrants, especially from Spain and Portugal, bound for new lives in Latin America. Companies such as the Hamburg-South America Line capitalized on this and built a fleet of fine passenger ships, including several large ones, specifically for this South Atlantic trade. One of these was the *Cap Polonio*, whose completion as a passenger ship had been halted in the summer of 1914 when the war broke out. She was later completed as the German Navy's armed cruiser *Vineta*. She proved unsuccessful, reverted to the name *Cap Polonio* and was soon laid up. In 1919, she was ceded to the British, going on to do service for the Union Castle and P&O Lines, but, rather strangely, without having her name changed. She was returned to Hamburg-South America in 1921 and refitted, finally entering service to Rio de Janeiro, Santos, Montevideo, and Buenos Aires. For a time she ranked as the finest European liner sailing to South America. She was a predecessor to the highly successful *Cap Arcona* of 1927, seen here at Hamburg (*below*) to the left. The *Cap Polonio* was a victim of the Depression. She was laid up in 1931, briefly served as an exhibition ship at Hamburg in 1933 and went to the breakers in 1935. [Built by Blohm & Voss Shipbuilders, Hamburg, Germany, 1914. 20,576 gross tons; 662 feet long; 72 feet wide. Steam triple expansion engines, triple screw. Service speed 17 knots. 1,555 passengers (356 first-class, 250 second-class, 949 third-class).]

THE 1920S: REVIVAL AND RENEWAL / 15

MONTE ROSA ~ The emigration trade, particularly from Spanish and Portugese ports to the east coast of South America, was immense. It prompted the Hamburg-South America Line to build five twin-funnel sisters. The *Monte Sarmiento* was first, commissioned in November 1924, followed by the *Monte Olivia* (1925), *Monte Cervantes* (1928), *Monte Pascoal* (1931), and finally *Monte Rosa* (1932), seen here during a summertime cruise in Norway's Geirangerfjord *(opposite, top)*. [Built by Blohm & Voss Shipbuilders, Hamburg, Germany, 1931. 13,882 gross tons; 524 feet long; 66 feet wide. M.A.N. diesels, twin screw. Service speed 14 knots. 2,408 passengers (1,372 tourist-class, 1,036 steerage).]

The *Monte Rosa* offered comfortable quarters in what was otherwise called third class *(opposite, middle)*. These were used for cruises, during which the very spartan steerage space was sealed off. The *Monte Rosa* and her sisters made cruises from Germany and the Netherlands to Norway, the Baltic, the British Isles, the Canary Islands, Spain, and Portugal, and into the Mediterranean. They were also frequently chartered by the Nazi government for so-called *Kraft durch Freude* ("Strength through Joy") cruises.

The *Monte Cervantes* and her sister ships were comparatively small, but their kitchens *(opposite, bottom)* prepared as many as 2,500 meals three times each day.

CAP ARCONA ~ Unquestionably, the *Cap Arcona*, seen here at Hamburg *(above)*, was the largest, fastest, and grandest German liner on the South American run. Few ships had greater popularity and acclaim, and her reputation lives on to this day. [Built by Blohm & Voss Shipbuilders, Hamburg, Germany, 1927. 27,560 gross tons; 676 feet long; 84 feet wide. Steam turbines, twin screw. Service speed 20 knots. 1,315 passengers (575 first-class, 275 second-class, 465 third-class).]

This ship's Winter Garden (*opposite, top*) included rattan chairs, potted palms and a vast stained-glass skylight overhead. It was often a delightful refuge from the changeable weather conditions during the 16-day voyage from Hamburg to Buenos Aires.

The first-class main hall (*opposite, middle*) had the elegant style and cozy splendor of a fine European hotel. Prosperous European businessmen mingled with their South American counterparts in a setting rich with the smell of tobacco, flowers, and polished woods.

The indoor pool (*opposite, bottom*) was a popular amenity, especially on warm-weather days in the South Atlantic. The ship was converted, however, into an accommodation vessel for the German Navy in 1940. The onetime queen of the South Atlantic was berthed for over four years in the port of Gdynia—renamed Gotenhafen by the Nazis—in occupied Poland. But sadly, a great tragedy awaited the *Cap Arcona*. She was activated in the winter of 1945 and evacuated some 26,000 people on three voyages from the German-occupied eastern territories, from which German forces were in rapid retreat. On her fourth trip, in April, she met her tragic end. "Some 5,000 prisoners from the Neuengamme concentration camp were embarked while the ship was off Neustadt in the Bay of Lübeck. There were now 6,000 people aboard, including crew and guards," according to Arnold Kludas. "On May 3, the *Cap Arcona* was attacked by British fighter-bombers and caught fire. Almost all means of rescue were destroyed by the rockets and the machine-gun fire from the aircraft. Panic broke out onboard, and shortly afterwards the *Cap Arcona* capsized. Although the ship was lying only a few hundred yards from shore, with a third of her width still out of the water, the disaster claimed 5,000 lives. The death of these thousands of concentration camp prisoners was all the more tragic since it came at the hands of those who would have liberated them only a few days later." The wreckage of the *Cap Arcona* was broken up where it lay in the late 1940s.

MILWAUKEE ~ In the 1920s, with promising times thought to be ahead, the Hamburg America Line, like others, built and planned new passenger ship tonnage. Two new liners were ordered for the North Atlantic service to New York, but also with an eye toward off-season cruising. The Germans had long used American names for their ships as a way of luring more passengers, especially US-bound Germans. The two new sister ships were named for cities noted for their German-American populations: the *Milwaukee*, seen (*above*) in the Geirangerfjord in Norway during a summer cruise from Hamburg, and the *St. Louis*. The *Milwaukee* was later repainted all in white and made over as a full-time cruise ship, which Hamburg America often insisted was "more like a floating health spa." [Built by Blohm & Voss Shipbuilders, Hamburg, Germany, 1929. 16,699 gross tons; 575 feet long; 72 feet wide. M.A.N. diesels, twin screw. Service speed 16 knots. 957 passengers (270 first-class, 259 tourist-class, 428 third-class).]

THE 1920S: REVIVAL AND RENEWAL / 19

The *Milwaukee*, seen here in dry dock while her propellers were being changed (*above*), survived the Second World War and was ceded to the British in 1945, only to burn a year later. The *St. Louis* is perhaps best remembered for her voyage in May–June 1939 from Hamburg to Cuba, with 900 Jewish refugees onboard. The Cuban authorities refused to accept them, as did the Americans. To the Nazi regime's pleasure, the ship was forced to return to Europe. Their attempt to prove that no one wanted to accept Jewish refugees was considered a propaganda success. The Belgians, British, French, and Dutch did later agree to accept them and they disembarked at Antwerp on June 17. Two months later, on August 26, the *St. Louis* fled New York due to the imminent war in Europe. She took a very northerly route back to Germany, even calling at Murmansk, finally reaching Hamburg on January 1, 1940. Idle for most of the war, she was bombed during the Allied air raid on Kiel in August 1944. Her partially damaged remains did serve a postwar purpose: she was a hotel in Hamburg harbor from 1946 until 1950. Two years later, she was broken up. [Built by Blohm & Voss Shipbuilders, Hamburg, Germany, 1929. 16,699 gross tons; 575 feet long; 72 feet wide. M.A.N. diesels, twin screw. Service speed 16 knots. 957 passengers (270 first-class, 259 tourist-class, 428 third-class).]

BERLIN (1925) ∼ Other intermediate-size ships used on the Atlantic by the Germans included the *Berlin* of North German Lloyd. She sailed between Bremerhaven and New York via Southampton and Cherbourg, and on occasional cruises. She made news when, on October 14, 1937, she sailed from New York's Pier 86 for Germany with a cargo of American scrap metal (*opposite, top*), presumably for Nazi munition factories. She made further news when, during a summer cruise in 1939, her boilers exploded. Seventeen crew members were killed. During the war, from 1940 until 1944, she served as a hospital ship, and then as an accommodation vessel in 1944–45. She hit a mine and sank off Swinemünde on February 1, 1945. She was salvaged by the Soviets in 1949 and began sailing again 1957 as the *Admiral Nakhimov* on the Black Sea coastal run out of Odessa. Her end was tragic. Following a collision with a Soviet cargo vessel in the Black Sea on August 31, 1986, she quickly sank, with the loss of 423 lives. It was the worst tragedy in peacetime Soviet maritime history. [Built by Bremer-Vulkan Shipyard, Bremen, Germany, 1925. 15,286 gross tons; 572 feet long; 69 feet wide. Steam triple expansion engines, twin screw. Service speed 16 knots. 1,122 passengers as built (220 first-class, 284 second-class, 618 third-class).]

MÜNCHEN ∼ Another of North German Lloyd's fine intermediate liners was the *München*, which was completed in the summer of 1923. Her first-class lounge (*opposite, bottom*) was a bright, cheerful space and included a glass skylight. Nearly lost during a fire at her New York City pier in February 1930, she was repaired and returned to Germany for rebuilding. She reemerged as the *General von Steuben* (shortened in 1938 to *Steuben*) and subsequently was used entirely for all-first-class cruising. She spent much of the war as a moored accommodation ship, but was revived in 1944 to carry wounded soldiers back to Germany from Baltic ports. On February 9, 1945, she left Pillau for Kiel on what would be her last, devastating voyage. She was carrying 2,500 wounded, 2,000 refugees, and 450 crew at the time. A day later, off Stolpmünde, she was hit with two torpedoes fired from a Soviet submarine. Some 3,000 perished. [Built by Vulcan Shipyard, Stettin, Germany, 1923. 13,325 gross tons; 551 feet long; 65 feet wide. Steam triple expansion engines, twin screw. Service speed 15 knots. 1,079 passengers as built (171 first-class, 350 second-class, 558 third-class).]

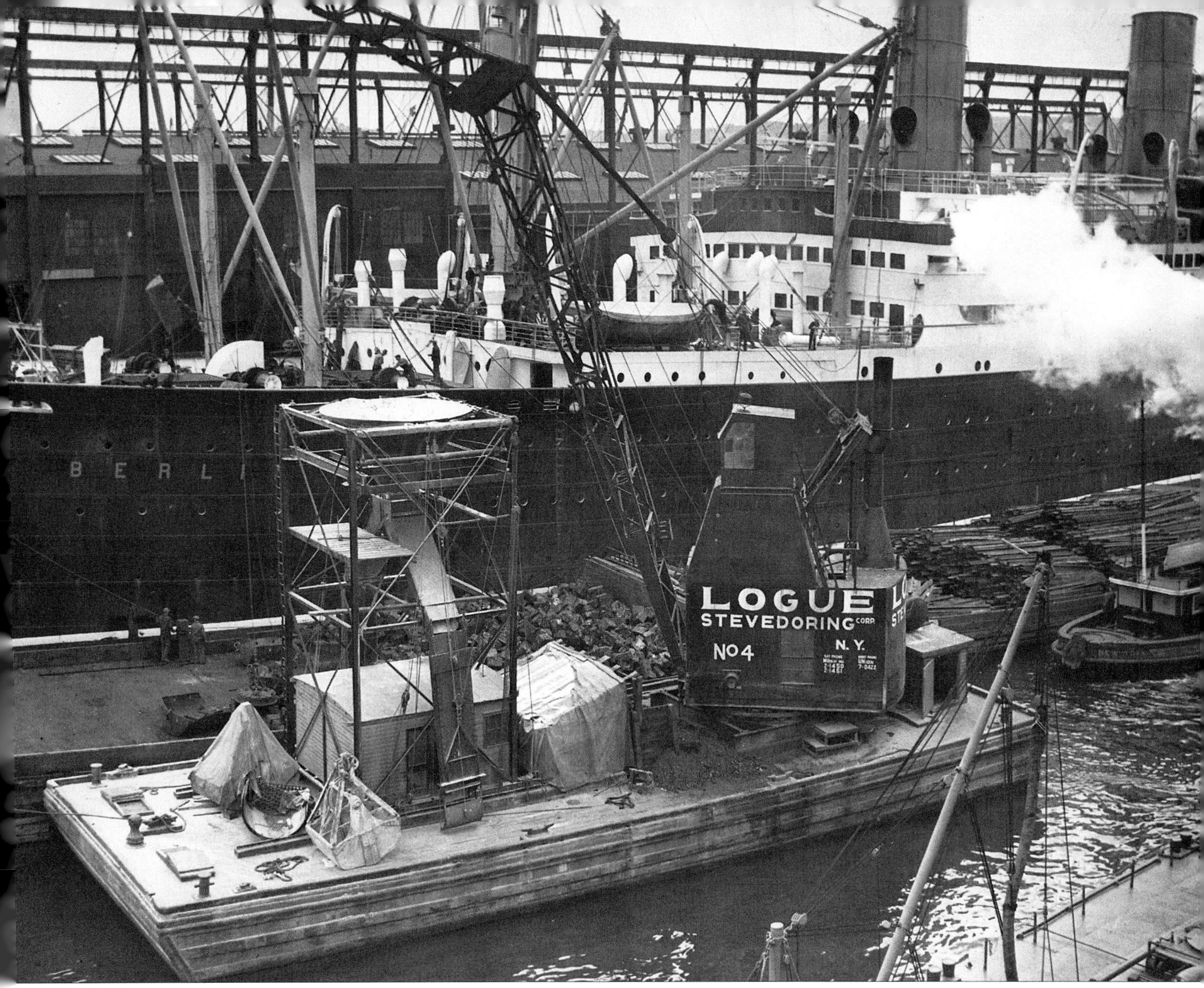
BERLI
LOGUE
STEVEDORING CORP.
No4
N.Y.

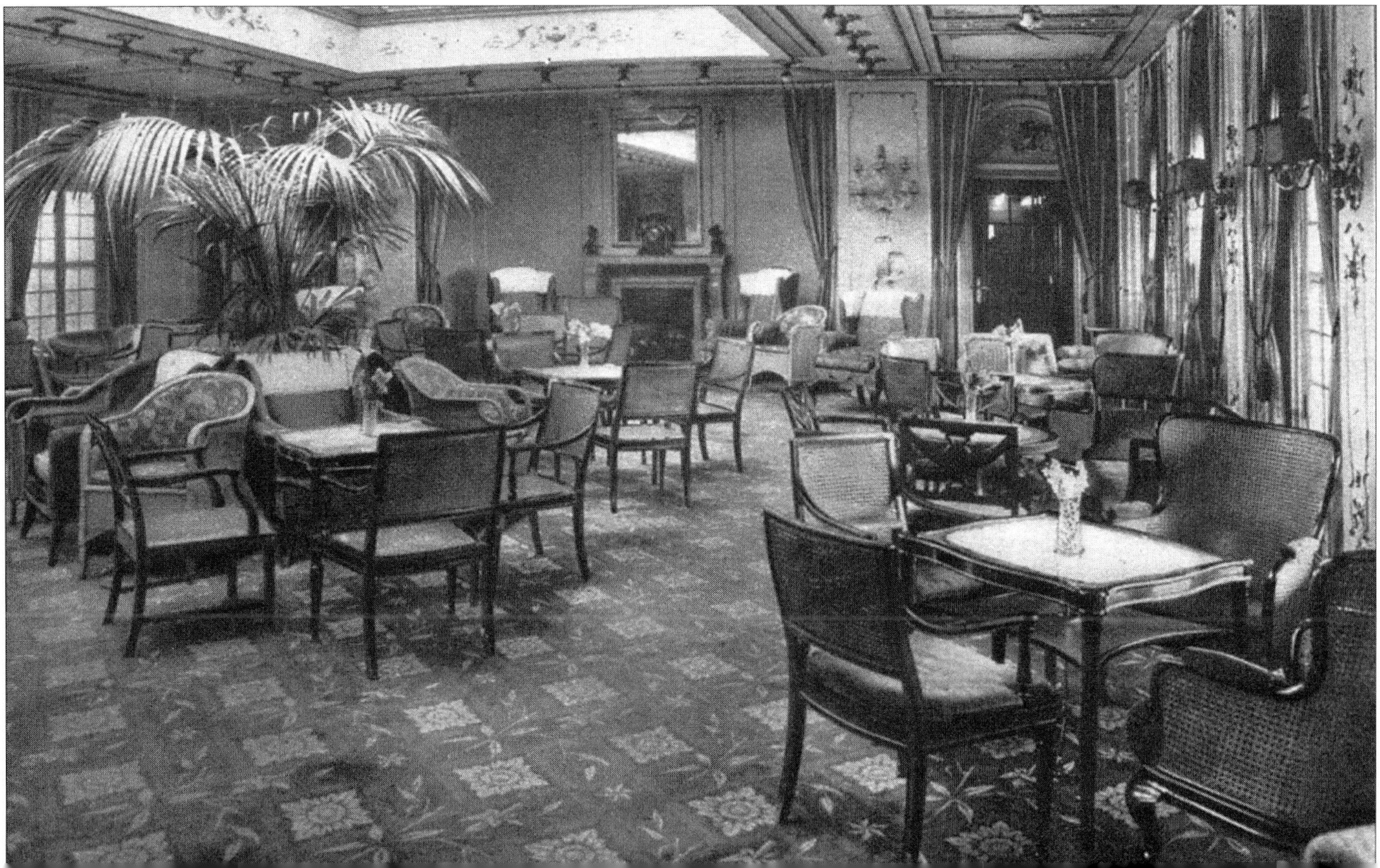

CHAPTER TWO

The 1930s: Economics, Politics and the Eve of War

In the spring of 1930, a largely unknown German actress arrived at New York for the first time. While she had had some success at Berlin's UFA Studio, it was the magical lure of Hollywood, in particular the great Paramount Studios, that drew her across the North Atlantic. Quickly, she became a major star, a worldwide celebrity, one of the great goddesses of Depression-era filmdom. Her name was Marlene Dietrich and she arrived aboard the *Bremen*, then the fastest liner afloat. At the time, the ship's owner, North German Lloyd, was using Pier 4 of the Brooklyn Army Terminal in the outer reaches of New York harbor. In retrospect, it seems a most unlikely location for the glamorous Dietrich to set her slender foot on American soil for the first time. Now, with the *Bremen* long gone (lost to fire in 1941) and Dietrich dead (in 1991), the story is complete: the old Army Terminal piers fell into ruins—two of the 1,800-foot-long docks collapsed and fell into the water—and in 1999 were demolished.

Built in 1919 and completed in record time, the Brooklyn Army Terminal was a product of the First World War and the US Government's need to greatly expand its postwar shipping capabilities. Helping to revive a war-ravaged Europe, lots of freighters used the terminal, a vast complex with offices, warehouses, and a system of railway tracks. Later, the Norwegian America Line, with passenger ships such as the *Bergensfjord* and *Stavangerfjord*, sublet part of it. North German Lloyd, unable to find an adequate berth at a more convenient Manhattan pier, also leased space there for about ten years, until 1934, when it was able to transfer its operations northward, to Pier 86 on the Hudson River at West 46th Street. Both of Lloyd's 1920s giants, the *Bremen* and *Europa*, had arrived at Brooklyn on their maiden voyages, and Lloyd publicists had worked hard to overcome the inconvenience of that Brooklyn terminal: "You are that much closer to Europe when you sail from Brooklyn on North German Lloyd liners to Europe!"

After World War II, the Terminal was used largely by the US Military Sea Transportation Service (MSTS), which ran a large fleet of peacetime troopships and transports to such transatlantic ports as Southampton, Bremerhaven, and Rota (in Spain), and to Puerto Rico, the Panama Canal Zone, and Labrador. Thousands of young soldiers went overseas for the first time from these Brooklyn piers. Perhaps the most famous departure was in 1958 when the *General G. M. Randall* departed for Germany. Waving farewell from the open deck was a young Elvis Presley. America shifted to air transport for all trooping by 1973 and soon afterward the Terminal itself closed. A freighter company, the Greek-flag Hellenic Lines, was the last to actually use the docks and the bankrupt cruise ship *Victoria* one of the last ships to tie up there, in the summer of 1975. By the late seventies, all that remained to hint of busier, bygone days was a faded military sign at the far end of Pier 4. It read: "Welcome Home."

In October 1998, New York City celebrated the works of architect Cass Gilbert. Among his creations were the Woolworth Building, the Federal Courthouse on Foley Square and the Brooklyn Army Terminal. On a Sunday afternoon, a chartered ferry took visitors to those old, forlorn docks. I wonder if anyone remembered Marlene Dietrich and the big German ocean liners.

BREMEN (1929) and EUROPA (1930) "In the first designs, they were intended to be 36,000 tons, just slightly larger than the *Columbus*. Then when they were ordered, the plans changed to 46,000 tons," according to Arnold Kludas. "But they were finished at 50,000 tons, two of the largest liners then afloat." North German Lloyd wanted to make a statement: it had survived the First World War and was regaining its prominence on the highly competitive North Atlantic run. More specifically, it would be powerful enough to take the prized Blue Ribbon away from the British Cunard veteran *Mauretania*, the world's fastest liner since 1907. The glory of the great German "floating palaces" would be revived. There was even a rumor that the Germans intended to have the two new superliners cross on their maiden voyages to New York at the same time and break the record together. The *Europa* was launched first, on August 15, 1928, at Hamburg; the *Bremen*, seen here (*above*), followed a day later, at Bremen. [Built by A. G. Weser Shipbuilders, Bremen, Germany, 1929. 51,656 gross tons; 938 feet long; 102 feet wide. Steam turbines, quadruple screw. Service speed 27 knots. 2,200 passengers (800 first-class, 500 second-class, 300 tourist-class, 600 third-class).]

The *Europa* was launched in the presence of German president von Hindenburg and the occasion was witnessed by thousands (*below*). [Built by Blohm & Voss Shipbuilders, Hamburg, Germany, 1930. 49,746 gross tons; 936 feet long; 102 feet wide. Steam turbines, quadruple screw. Service speed 27 knots. 2,024 passengers (687 first-class, 524 second-class, 306 tourist-class, 507 third-class).]

24 / THE 1930S: ECONOMICS, POLITICS AND THE EVE OF WAR

The *Europa* was to have been the first of the pair to enter service, in the late spring of 1929. On March 26, 1929, however, fire swept the new liner at her Hamburg shipyard berth. The damages were so extensive (*opposite, top*) that it was first reported that she might have to be scrapped. But resourceful Blohm & Voss engineers saved the day. The *Europa* was repaired, but was launched a year late.

The *Bremen* (*opposite, bottom*), seen here undergoing repairs in the big floating dry dock at Blohm & Voss in Hamburg, therefore became the first to enter service. She left Bremerhaven on her maiden crossing to New York on July 16, 1929. With stops at Southampton and Cherbourg, it was a triumphant trip. The *Bremen* captured the Blue Ribbon with a speed of 27.83 knots (beating *Mauretania*'s 26.6, dating from 1909). The German liner's passage took 4 days, 17 hours, 42 minutes. The struggling *Mauretania* tried once more, making an incredible 27.2 knots despite her 22 years of age, but in the end could not succeed. Instead, the Cunarder sent warmest congratulations to her new Germanic successor. Berlin beamed with pride.

Even before they were launched, the two new superships were already well known to Germans. According to Arnold Kludas, when North German Lloyd ordered the ships in 1926, it expected to finance them with government help, but the money never materialized. The ships were successful, but in the worldwide Depression, Lloyd struggled financially. In 1933 the new government of the Third Reich, which treated the steamship companies as bearers of national prestige, took control of the company.

The *Bremen* and *Europa* in service. The long, inconvenient Pier 4 at the Brooklyn Army Terminal was located near the lower end of New York harbor (*below*). In this view, the *Bremen* is on the left; the *Columbus* is angled slightly in the upper right berth with the *Karlsruhe* just behind her.

THE 1930S: ECONOMICS, POLITICS AND THE EVE OF WAR / 25

The two big Lloyd liners quickly became known for their reliability, their impeccable maintenance, and their crisp service. Their gala midnight sailings from New York were also celebrated: with funnels aglow, names spelled out in lights, and a roaring German band playing on deck, the ships sailed down the harbor with the twinkling windows of the Manhattan skyline as a backdrop. The lighted letters (*right*) were two meters high and were illuminated by 1,200 electric lamps.

Lloyd publicists worked especially hard to keep the *Bremen* and the *Europa* in the news. One of these ships' great novelties was the small seaplane in a revolving catapult on the top deck. When either ship neared New York or Southampton, the plane could be sent off with a few bags of mail and maybe a special passenger, to arrive ahead of the ship (*middle*). It was a rather expensive, bothersome, and even clumsy process, but extremely important for publicity.

"The *Bremen* and *Europa* worked well, especially considering there was the Great Depression in their first years," says Arnold Kludas. "But soon they had serious rivals, other superliners like the *Rex*, the *Normandie*, and the *Queen Mary*. By 1934–35, the German liners were not grabbing as many passengers. Of course, by then, there was anti-Nazi sentiment. By the late 1930s, the two big ships were never full-up." Here we see the *Europa* encountering some brisk weather in the North Atlantic (*bottom*).

The first-class social rooms aboard the *Europa* were among the ship's most impressive spaces. A Lloyd brochure noted, "The social rooms form a long flight of halls on the main promenade deck. The Smoking Room with Verandah, the imposing lounge (*top*) measuring 40 meters in length, the Art Saloon, the Library and Writing Room, and the Ballroom compete with another in beauty."

Extreme coziness is the characteristic note of the *Europa*'s Smoking Room," (*middle*) said one German magazine in May 1930. "Macassar ebony paneling, pigskin wall covering, handsome marble fireplaces and artistic curtains and fabrics for the furnishings produce a beautiful color effect. Hunting and sport scenes add to the charm of the room."

Peak summer season fares in 1937 for the two German giants for the six-day crossings between New York and Bremerhaven were placed at $255 in first class, $129 in second class, and $89 in third class. Comparatively, Hapag-Lloyd, which was the New York agent for the giant zeppelin *Hindenburg*, posted fares for the three-day passage at $400 per person. Here we see the living-dining area of a first-class cabin deluxe on the *Europa* (*bottom*).

27

28 / The 1930s: Economics, Politics and the Eve of War

The top decks on the *Bremen*, seen here *(opposite, top)*, seem to tower above the open seas while a view on the *Europa* shows guests taking their daily exercise *(opposite, bottom)*.

There was one problem with these German giants. Their squat funnels, which gave them a long, lean look, "almost like sea monsters," said one onlooker, were inefficient. Smoke and soot fell onto the aft passenger decks. Soon, the funnels on both ships were raised, giving them a far more powerful, imposing look. The *Europa* is especially majestic-looking in this view *(right)* as she closely passes another German passenger ship.

The Depression prompted many companies to merge or at least better coordinate their duplicate services, especially on the North Atlantic run to New York. In 1931, the Hamburg America Line and North German Lloyd joined their operations under the name Hapag-Lloyd. At New York, they shared terminals as well. In this view *(below)* dated April 22, 1934, the *Bremen* is to the left, occupying Pier 86 at West 46th Street, while the *Hamburg* (center) and the *Reliance* share Pier 84.

By the late 1930s, the *Bremen* and *Europa* were less popular with Americans, particularly with American Jews, but retained some European following, especially among Germans. As "ships of state," however, like Italy's *Rex* and France's *Normandie*, they had not been built in the unrealistic expectation of high profitability, but as grandiose ornaments, symbols of national pride and ability. In this view, two crew members of the *Europa* stand guard alongside the swastika, the Nazi Party's emblem, on August 1, 1935 (*above*). It was the first time that the ship had arrived in New York flying the Nazi colors. A week before, the *Bremen* had been invaded prior to a midnight sailing by a "mob of Communists" (according to the New York *Daily News*), who ripped down the Nazi flag and threw it into the Hudson River.

The war and after. The *Bremen* was delayed at Pier 86 on August 28–29, 1939 (*right*). With war in Europe close at hand, her scheduled commercial trip was canceled. "She was held all day while Customs searches combed the entire ship looking for contraband," writes ship historian Frank Cronican. "All available inspectors reported for searching duty. All holds and passenger quarters as well as crew areas were searched. The ship was held all night and one extra day. Another search was started the next day [the 29th]." Finally cleared, the liner was allowed to sail, but under strict orders from Berlin. At sea, she was repainted in grays and "blacked out" at night. She took a very northerly course, reaching Murmansk on September 6. Slowly, she made her way south, hiding in fog banks and clinging to the Norwegian coast. She even raised the Soviet colors for a time as a precaution against British attack. She reached Bremerhaven on December 13, and never sailed again. Considered for use as a troop transport for the intended Nazi invasion of England or for possible conversion to an aircraft carrier, she sat idle. On March 16, 1941, a young crewman, unhappy with the Nazis, set her afire. She later capsized. Her remains were cut up for scrap for the German war effort; the very last pieces were taken to a lower part of the Weser River and deliberately sunk.

30 / THE 1930S: ECONOMICS, POLITICS AND THE EVE OF WAR

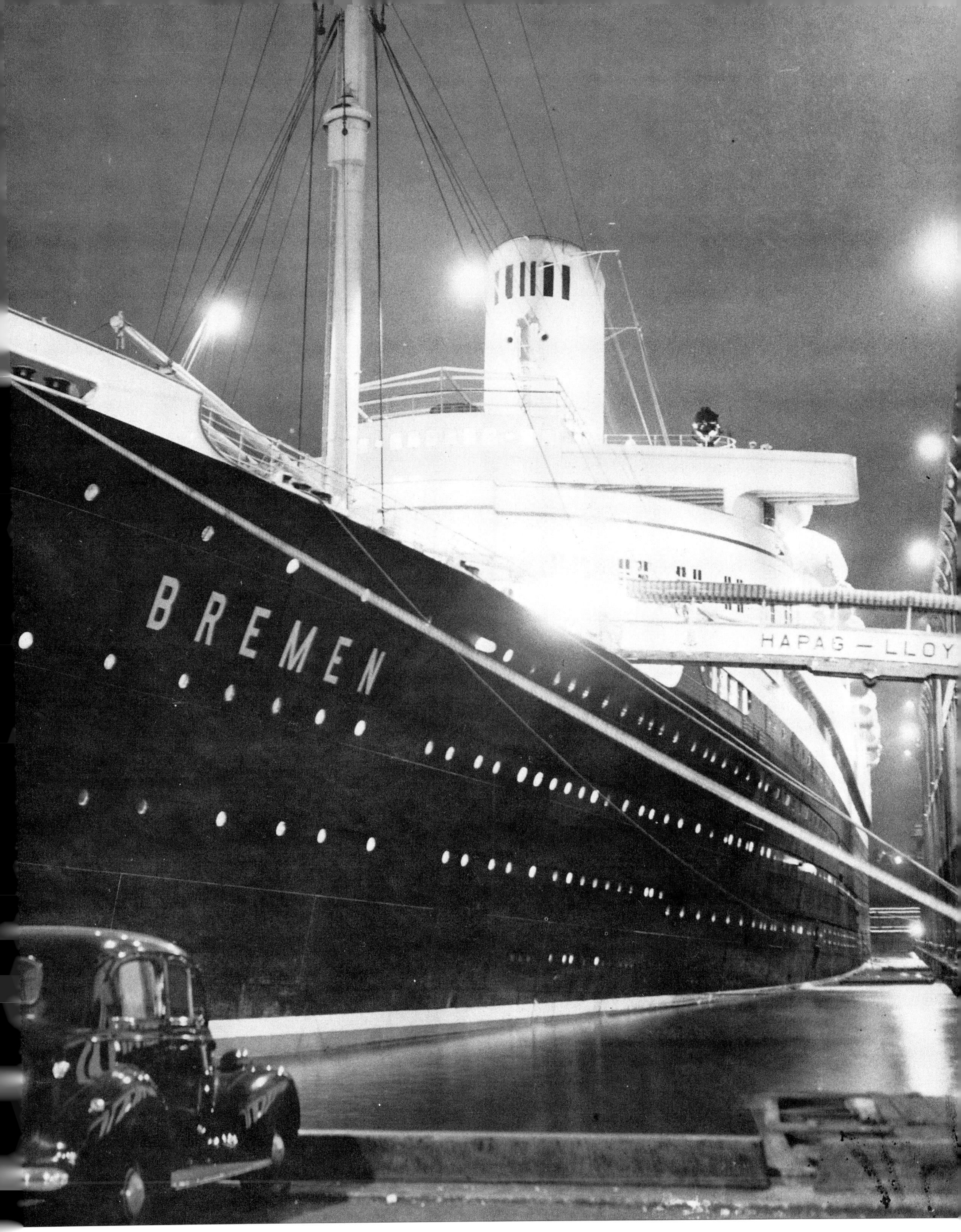
BREMEN
HAPAG — LLOY

The *Europa* fared better. Left at Bremerhaven for the duration of the war, she was seized by invading American forces in May 1945 and revived as a troopship under the name USS *Europa*. But plagued with problems, including many small fires, she was given as reparations to the French in 1946. After thorough reconditioning (she is seen here in the final stages, on July 12, 1950, at a shipyard at St. Nazaire), she resumed Atlantic sailings as the *Liberté* for the French Line in August 1950 (*above*). The last of the German giants, she was retired in November 1961 and soon afterward sold to Italian shipbreakers. The former *Europa* finished her long and distinguished career in the quiet harbor at La Spezia, not far from Genoa, in the spring of 1962.

PATRIA (1919) Apart from Atlantic service to North America, the Dutch had fleets of passenger ships supporting their colonial links to the Dutch East Indies (now Indonesia) and to the Dutch West Indies (Curaçao, Aruba) and South America (Surinam). Rotterdam Lloyd and the Nederland Line, based at Rotterdam and Amsterdam respectively, dominated passenger services to the East. They had built successively larger ships, always passenger-and-cargo, for the long voyages to and from the tropics. Government officials, merchants, traders, missionaries, and families steadily filled their berths. The *Patria* (*opposite, top*) was one of the largest ships on this run in the 1920s. She had been ordered in 1914 for delivery in 1915, but was delayed by the war and not completed until 1919. Her itinerary read: Rotterdam, Southampton, Lisbon, Gibraltar, Marseilles, Port Said, Colombo, Sabang, Belawan Deli, Singapore, and Batavia (Jakarta). Her long voyages were eased somewhat when, in 1927, a special train, the *Rotterdam Lloyd Rapide*, started a service between Rotterdam and Marseilles with stops at Antwerp, Brussels, and Paris. The passage took 22 hours, compared to five days by sea. The train was especially useful to the Dutch coming home on leave after long stints in the East Indies. The Depression of the 1930s wreaked havoc even on the colonial services, however. The number of outbound passengers dropped by as much as 50 percent, and freight declined even more. Special low-fare tourist excursions were offered to Lisbon to recruit at least a few vacationers ($44 for the five-day voyage) and student cruises to the Norwegian fjords were organized for summer. Companies like Rotterdam Lloyd had to scrap some older ships just to build one or two new ones. The *Patria* herself was laid up prematurely in 1934, and soon sold to the Soviets, who renamed her *Svir*. Sunk at Leningrad during the Second World War, she was later salvaged and repaired, and sailed out of Vladivostock until scrapped at Hong Kong in 1979. [Built by De Schelde Shipyard, Flushing, Netherlands, 1919. 9,891 gross tons; 480 feet long; 57 feet wide. Steam turbines, twin screw. Service speed 17 knots. 332 passengers (120 first-class, 124 second-class, 44 third-class, 44 fourth-class).]

32 / THE 1930s: ECONOMICS, POLITICS AND THE EVE OF WAR

SIBAJAK ⁓ Another of the colonial Dutch East Indian ships was the *Sibajak*. Her first class bar-lounge (**middle**) shows the decor typical of these colonial liners. The *Sibajak*'s long career with the Dutch, which included trooping service with the British during World War II, postwar duties carrying emigrants to Australia and even some transatlantic crossings for the Holland America Line, ended at a Hong Kong scrapyard in 1959. [Built by De Schelde Shipyard, Flushing, Netherlands, 1925. 12,040 gross tons; 530 feet long; 62 feet wide. Sulzer diesels, twin screw. Service speed 17 knots. 454 passengers (212 first-class, 174 second-class, 68 third-class).]

INSULINDE ⁓ This first-class cabin (**bottom**) was priced at $450 for the 30-day voyage from Rotterdam to Batavia (Jakarta). The *Insulinde* was another victim of the Depression. She was laid up and soon sold to the French line Compagnie Générale de Navigation Vapeur, which sailed her as the *Banfora* until 1957. Her very last trip, from Marseilles to scrappers in Yokohama, was as the *Banfora Maru*. [Built by De Schelde Shipyard, Flushing, Netherlands, 1912. 9,615 gross tons; 480 feet long; 57 feet wide. Steam triple expansion engines, twin screw. Service speed 15 knots. 303 passengers (111 first-class, 112 second-class, 40 third-class, 40 fourth-class).]

THE 1930S: ECONOMICS, POLITICS AND THE EVE OF WAR / 33

34 / THE 1930S: ECONOMICS, POLITICS AND THE EVE OF WAR

NIEUW HOLLAND ~ For local and short sea routes in the East, the Dutch built a vast fleet of small passenger ships. The largest of these, the sisters *Nieuw Holland* (**opposite, top**) and *Nieuw Zeeland*, sailed between Java and Australia. Their exact itinerary in the late 1930s was from Singapore to Batavia, Semerang, Surabaya, Brisbane, Sydney, Melbourne, and Adelaide. From Singapore to Adelaide took four weeks. Once these ships were completed, they never returned to the Netherlands. Operated by the Dutch Koninklijke Pakevaart Mij, the KPM Line, based in Batavia, the *Nieuw Zeeland* was lost in the Second World War while the *Nieuw Holland* went on to sail for the reorganized Royal Interocean Lines, another Dutch company, until broken up in 1959. [Built by Netherlands Shipbuilding Company, Amsterdam, Netherlands, 1928. 10,903 gross tons; 527 feet long; 62 feet wide. Steam turbines, twin screw. Service speed 15 knots. 173 passengers (123 first-class, 50 third-class).]

CHRISTIAAN HUYGENS ~ The *Christiaan Huygens* (**opposite, bottom**) was one of the largest and finest liners on the Dutch East Indies trade when she was completed in the winter of 1928. She appeared to be longer than she actually was, especially in that she had a very small, almost paint-can-like single stack. She very much reflected the lean, spare design popular for new liners in the late 1920s and early 30s. In consideration of her long tropical voyages, she was also sensibly designed with a great amount of open deck space. Used as a trooper by the British beginning in 1940, she survived the Second World War, but less than two weeks after V-J Day, on August 26, 1945, on a short voyage from Antwerp to Rotterdam, she struck an unmarked mine off the Dutch coast. Beached and badly damaged, she later broke in half and had to be scrapped. [Built by Netherlands Shipbuilding & Dry Dock Company, Amsterdam, Netherlands, 1928. 15,637 gross tons; 570 feet long; 68 feet wide. Sulzer diesels, twin screw. Service speed 16.5 knots. 572 passengers (269 first-class, 250 second-class, 53 third-class).]

JOHAN VAN OLDENBARNEVELT ~ The design of the *Christiaan Huygens* led to a pair of even bigger, slightly superior ships for the Nederland Line's Amsterdam–East Indies trade. Having a similar low, flat design but with two funnels instead of one, the *Johan van Oldenbarnevelt* was commissioned in the spring of 1930, her sister, the *Marnix van St Aldegonde*, the following autumn. They were two of the finest and most popular Dutch liners. The ships were routed from Amsterdam and Southampton to Batavia via Gibraltar or Algiers, Palma or Villefranche, Genoa, Port Said, Colombo, Sebang, Belawan Deli, and Singapore. First-class fare for the four-week trip from Amsterdam to Batavia started at $400. Third-class rates began at $200. The *Johan van Oldenbarnevelt* is seen here arriving at Belawan Deli on Sumatra (**above**). The *Marnix van St Aldegonde* was a war casualty, sunk by German bombers off Algeria in November 1943; fortunately, all her 3,000 troops were rescued. [Built by Netherlands Shipbuilding & Dry Dock Company, Amsterdam, Netherlands, 1930. 19,040 gross tons; 608 feet long; 74 feet wide. Sulzer diesels, twin screw. Service speed 17 knots. 770 passengers (364 first-class, 280 second-class, 64 third-class, 62 fourth-class).]

The decor onboard the *Johan van Oldenbarnevelt* was meant to remind travelers, at least those in first class, of the Netherlands. For the most part, these were colonial administrative officials and their families, spice traders and merchants, and prosperous plantation owners. The music salon (*below*) was adorned with intricately carved wood panels, stained-glass windows, and a wall-mounted tapestry behind the orchestra stand. It was the perfect setting for afternoon teas and evening concerts.

During World War II, the JVO, as she was more commonly called, traveled extensively: 33 voyages, 281,000 miles, and some 72,000 passengers. She visited such places as Iceland and India, Suez and South Africa. However, she had a weakness: her engines. In June 1943, she was laid up at Liverpool for eleven months for much-needed repairs. In August 1945, she was to sail to Amsterdam, her first visit in over five years, but the call had to wait, as the North Lock of the North Sea Canal had been damaged by the retreating Nazis. In 1951, the JVO was rebuilt as shown (*opposite, top*) for emigrant service, mostly from Amsterdam to Fremantle, Melbourne, and Sydney, Australia. Her original four-class configuration for some 770 was made over for 1,414 all in one class. Cabins were rearranged as well, with very few double and triple rooms, but 200 four-berth cabins, 50 cabins with five or six berths and 13 large dormitories. All the rooms were fitted with washstands and cold running water only. New public amenities included a movie theater, a beauty salon and two passenger laundries.

In the winter of 1959, the JVO was again refitted, this time for all-tourist-class, around-the-world service. Her accommodations were improved with air conditioning, a second pool and some private plumbing in the cabins. She was routed on three-month eastabout itineraries: from Amsterdam and Southampton to Palma de Majorca, Genoa, Port Said, Suez, Colombo, Fremantle, Melbourne, Sydney, Wellington (*opposite, bottom*), Auckland, Suva, Papeete, Callao, Cristobal, Port Everglades, occasionally New York, and then homeward to Southampton and Amsterdam. Unfortunately, this new service was unsuccessful and her last with the Nederland Line. She was sold to the Greek Line and renamed *Lakonia* in the winter of 1963 and made over for cruising on 12- to 16-day voyages out of Southampton. But this new career was very brief. During a Christmas cruise, on December 22, 1963, she caught fire near Madeira. The blaze spread and the ship was abandoned and left adrift. Attempts to tow her later failed, and on December 29, she heeled over and sank.

36 / THE 1930S: ECONOMICS, POLITICS AND THE EVE OF WAR

THE 1930s: ECONOMICS, POLITICS AND THE EVE OF WAR / 37

38

BALOERAN ~ The shipping trade has always been a competitive business. Soon after its rival Nederland Line contracted for its two newest and largest ships, the aforementioned *Johan van Oldenbarnevelt* and *Marnix van St Aldegonde*, Rotterdam Lloyd ordered its largest and most luxurious passenger ships yet, the sisters *Baloeran* (**opposite, top**) and *Dempo*. There were problems of all sorts with the building of these ships. Only the *Baloeran*'s hull could be built by the Wilton-Fijenoord yard at Schiedam because the locks at Flushing were not large enough for such a ship. The hull had to be towed to another yard, the De Schelde plant, for completion. Delivered in 1930 and 1931 respectively, the two sisters could not have arrived at less opportune time. Trading, even to the colonies in the East Indies, had dropped drastically as the Depression set in in earnest. Four Rotterdam Lloyd freighters were sold to the breakers to make way for the new liners. Other, older passenger ships would not be replaced but upgraded. By late 1931, one third of the entire Dutch merchant marine was laid up. A year later, the once busy mail run to Batavia was reduced to four passenger ships and over a dozen cargo sailings went empty on voyages to the East. The *Baloeran* and *Dempo* became noted for their luxury quarters and eventually gained in popularity.

In September 1939, as war erupted, their Amsterdam-Suez-Batavia sailings were diverted to Genoa, where a train carried passengers to and from the Netherlands. Both ships became wartime casualties. The *Baloeran* fell into Nazi hands and became the hospital ship *Strassburg*, managed by the Hamburg America Line. She was mined off the Dutch coast in September 1943 and later lost. The *Dempo*, run by the British as a troopship, was torpedoed off North Africa in March 1944. [Built by Wilton-Fijenoord Shipyard, Schiedam, Netherlands, 1930. 16,981 gross tons; 573 feet long; 70 feet wide. Sulzer diesels, twin screw. Service speed 18 knots. 634 passengers (236 first-class, 280 second-class, 70 third-class, 48 fourth-class).]

This deluxe first class cabin on the *Dempo* (**opposite, middle**) included a bedroom, sitting area, and full bath.

COLOMBIA ~ Royal Netherlands Steamship Company, another Dutch company (often known by its Dutch initials KNSM), ran passenger services from both the Netherlands and New York to the Caribbean and South America. The European routing was triangular: Amsterdam and Dover to Madeira, then Paramaribo, Demarara, Trinidad, Carupano, Guanta, La Guaira, Maracaibo, Aruba, Curaçao, Puerto Cabello, and Port-au-Prince, then north to New York before reversing course on the same itinerary. Amsterdam to La Guaira took approximately 21 days, to New York about 28 days. One of the ships used on this service by the late 1930s was the *Colombia*, seen here (**opposite, bottom**) berthed at the Royal Netherlands terminal in Brooklyn Heights. The date is autumn 1939 and the ship is soon to be called to military duties. [Built by P. Smit, Jr. Shipyard, Rotterdam, Netherlands, 1930. 10,782 gross tons; 429 feet long; 61 feet wide. Diesels, twin screw. Service speed 15 knots. 240 passengers in three classes.]

CORDILLERA ~ Hapag-Lloyd's passenger services seemed to span the globe by the 1930s. On the Caribbean run, the passenger service was strengthened by two superb new liners, the *Cordillera* (**above**) and her twin sister, the *Caribia*. They operated out of Hamburg, Antwerp, Boulogne, and Dover to Barbados, Trinidad, La Guaira, Curaçao, Puerto Colombia, Cartagena, and Cristobal, reversed the same itinerary through the Caribbean, and then sailed to Plymouth, Cherbourg, and Amsterdam before returning to Hamburg. The full voyage took approximately 60 days. The 11 days from Hamburg to Barbados was priced at $160 in first class, $100 in second class and $72 in third class. [Built by Blohm & Voss Shipbuilders, Hamburg, Germany, 1933. 12,055 gross tons; 524 feet long; 65 feet wide. M.A.N. diesels, twin screw. Service speed 17 knots. 419 passengers (206 first-class, 103 second-class, 110 tourist-class).]

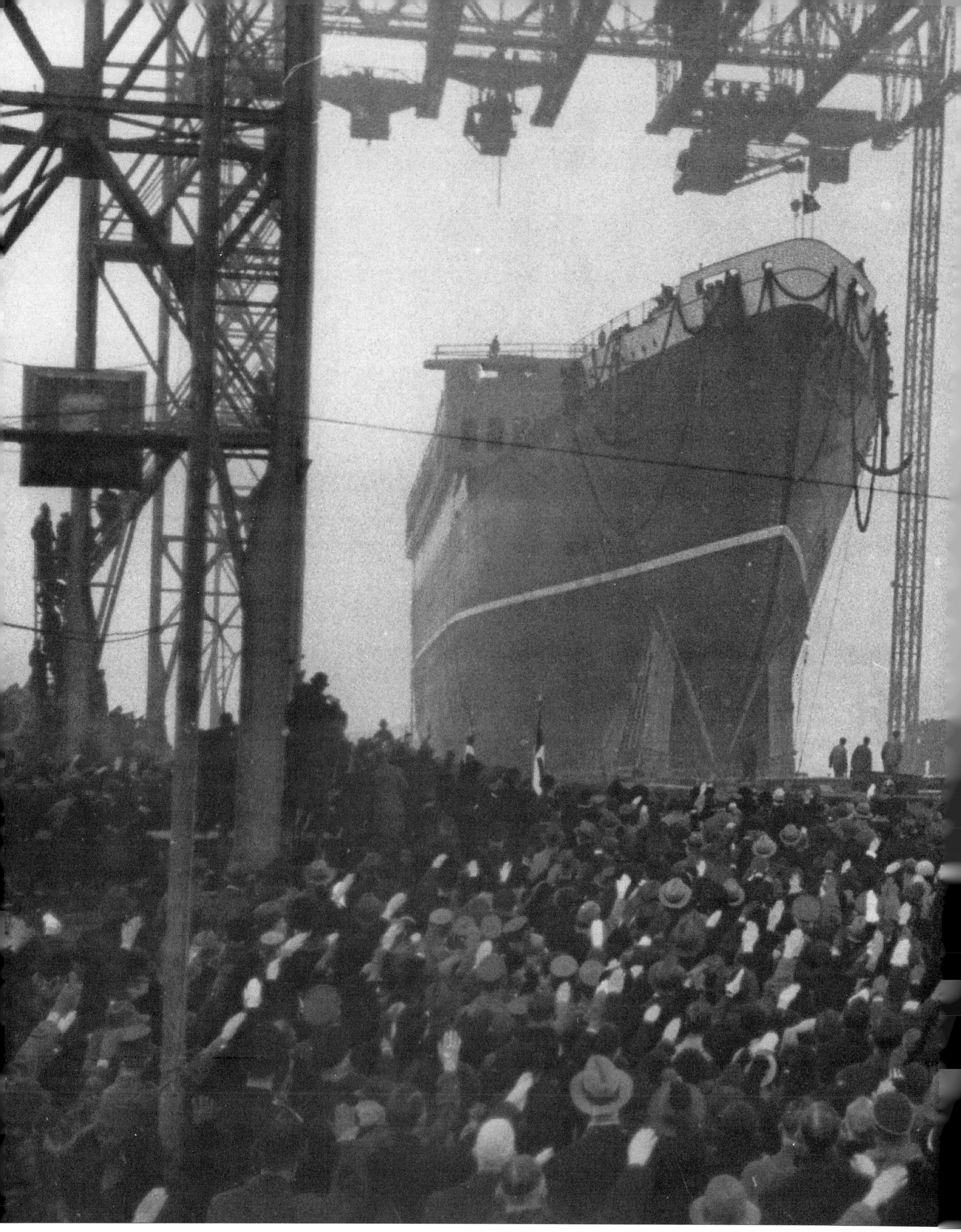

SCHARNHORST and GNEISENAU ~ "Both the Hamburg America Line and the North German Lloyd were practically state-controlled from 1930–31. This control passed to the Nazis by 1933," notes Arnold Kludas. "Plans were made with political implications. The two companies had to ask the Government to build new tonnage. Three new, large, very powerful passenger-cargo liners were built for the long-distance Far East trade, but they were created merely to impress the Japanese. Fast ships, they were symbols of German technology. In reality, they were quite useless, quite impractical. Similarly, the Nazis insisted on building another large combination liner, the *Patria*, which they wanted to be the very best ship on the run from Europe to the west coast of South America."

The three ships for the Far East were the *Scharnhorst*, shown here (*left*) being launched in the presence of Adolf Hitler on December 14, 1934, the *Gneisenau*, and the *Potsdam*. The first two were built for North German Lloyd, and the third was ordered by the Hamburg America Line but sold to North German Lloyd soon after her launching in January 1935. [Built by A. G. Weser Shipbuilders, Bremen, Germany, 1935. 18,184 gross tons; 652 feet long; 74 feet wide. Steam turbo-electric, twin screw. Service speed 21 knots. 293 passengers (149 first-class, 144 second-class).]

The three German Far East liners, including the *Gneisenau*, shown here *(above)*, were routed on six-week voyages from Hamburg to Yokohama and Kobe, with calls en route at Bremen, Antwerp, Southampton, Palma de Majorca, Barcelona, Genoa, Port Said, Suez, Colombo, Singapore, Manila, Hong Kong, and Shanghai. First-class fares for the full voyage started at $425 in 1938. [Built by A. G. Weser Shipbuilders, Bremen, Germany, 1935. 18,160 gross tons; 651 feet long; 74 feet wide. Steam turbines, twin screw. Service speed 21 knots. 293 passengers (149 first-class, 144 second-class).]

The three "German-Asia" liners, as they were sometimes called, were known for their superb quarters, especially in first class. Here we see the first-class main lounge *(opposite, top)* and bar *(opposite, bottom)* on the *Scharnhorst*. The three ships saw only a few years of commercial service with the Germans. Laid up in Japan in September 1939, the *Scharnhorst* was later sold to the Japanese Navy, rebuilt as the aircraft carrier *Shinyo* in 1942, and then sunk by an American submarine off the Chinese coast in November 1944. The *Gneisenau* was to have been converted to an aircraft carrier by the Nazis in 1942, but this never came to pass. She was mined and sunk in May 1943. The *Potsdam* became a British prize of war in June 1945 and became the troopship *Empire Jewel* and later *Empire Fowey*. In 1960, she was sold to Pakistani buyers and became the Muslim pilgrim ship *Safina-e-Hujjaj*. She was scrapped in Pakistan in 1976.

43

WINDHUK and PRETORIA ∼ "The *Windhuk* and *Pretoria* (*above*) were very luxurious on the inside. They catered not only to Germans living in east and west Africa, but also to many European and British passengers," notes Arnold Kludas. "They were also the last German liners to be built for African service. After the Second World War, the French and the Portugese had taken over the African trades. In addition, since 1941, shares in the German-Africa Line had been taken by a private German cigarette company and others, and each of whom were not interested in passenger shipping. Furthermore, Germans were not permitted to operate passenger ships until the 1950s and so the immediate postwar concentration was on freighters. German-Africa Line never resumed its passenger service." The largest liners belonging to the German-Africa Line, the *Windhuk* and the *Pretoria* sailed on that company's main service from Hamburg, Antwerp, Rotterdam, and Southampton via Las Palmas to Capetown, Port Elizabeth, East London, Durban, and Lourenço Marques. Fares for the 17-day voyage from Hamburg to Capetown were fixed at $200 for first class and $100 for tourist class. Neither ship remained with the Germans after the war. The *Windhuk* disguised herself as a Japanese liner, the *Santos Maru*, to avoid capture in the South Atlantic in the fall of 1939, and later fled to Brazil for safety. Seized by the Brazilian government, she was sold to the US Navy in 1942 and became the troopship USS *Lejeune*. Laid up from 1948 until 1966, she was then broken up in Oregon. The *Pretoria*, used as an accommodation ship by the Nazis during the war years, was seized by the British in 1945 and renamed *Empire Doon* and then in 1949 *Empire Orwell*. She sailed as a peacetime troopship under charter to the British Ministry of Transport until sold in 1958 to the Blue Funnel Line, also British, and refitted as the Muslim pilgrim ship *Gunung Djati*. She was sold to Indonesia in 1962, but retained her name. In 1979, she became the training ship *Tanjung Pandan* for the Indonesian Navy. She was finally scrapped on Taiwan in 1987 at the age of fifty-one. [Built by Blohm & Voss Shipbuilders, Hamburg, Germany, 1937. 16,662 gross tons; 577 feet long; 72 feet wide. Steam turbines, twin screw. Service speed 18 knots. 490 passengers (152 first-class, 338 tourist-class).]

USARAMO ~ The German-Africa Line ran a number of smaller passenger ships on the Europe-Africa run as well. Here we see the inbound *Usaramo* (**opposite, bottom**), arriving at Hamburg with the British cruise ship *Voltaire* to the left. [Built by Blohm & Voss Shipbuilders, Hamburg, Germany, 1920. 7,775 gross tons; 418 feet long; 56 feet wide. Steam turbines, single screw. Service speed 14 knots. 250 passengers in three classes.]

ADOLPH WOERMANN ~ The accommodations on the German-Africa Line passenger ships carried the typical stylings of, say, a small German hotel to the exotic ports of distant Africa. Here we see the first-class main hall (**above**) and the second-class dining room (**below**) aboard the *Adolph Woermann*. [Built by Reiherstieg Schiffwerft, Hamburg, Germany, 1906. 6,257 gross tons; 411 feet long; 50 feet wide. Steam triple expansion engines, twin screw. Service speed 13 knots. 204 passengers (102 first-class, 82 second-class, 20 third-class).]

THE 1930s: ECONOMICS, POLITICS AND THE EVE OF WAR / 45

46 / THE 1930S: ECONOMICS, POLITICS AND THE EVE OF WAR

PATRIA (1938) / ROSSIA ∽ The *Patria* was Germany's finest liner on the long-haul service from Hamburg to Valparaiso via the Panama Canal. It traveled from Hamburg, Bremen, and Antwerp to Cristobal, Buenaventura, Guayaquil, Callao, Mollendo, Arica, Antofagasta, and finally Valparaiso. A complete one-way voyage took approximately 35 days. Used by the German Navy during the Second World War, she was seized by the invading British forces in the spring of 1945 and became the troopship *Empire Welland*. There was a change of mind, however, and within a year the ship was given to the Soviets, who refitted her as the passenger liner *Rossia*. She made several Odessa–New York voyages—she is seen here docking at Staten Island in 1947 *(opposite, top)*—but was soon transferred to Black Sea coastal service out of Odessa. Later in her career, she made some crossings from Odessa to Havana. Sold to shipbreakers at Gadani Beach in Pakistan in 1985, she was temporarily renamed *Aniva* for the last voyage out from Odessa. [Built by Deutsche Werft, Hamburg, Germany, 1938. 16,595 gross tons; 598 feet long; 73 feet wide. Diesel-electric, twin screw. Service speed 17 knots. 349 passengers (185 first-class, 164 tourist-class).]

MAGDALENA ∽ Hamburg America's *Magdalena* ran aground at Curaçao in the Caribbean in February 1934 *(opposite, bottom)*. Eventually refloated and returned to Germany, she was soon rebuilt as the single-funnel *Iberia*. [Built by F. Schichau, Danzig, 1928. 9,779 gross; 466 feet long; 60 feet wide. M.A.N. diesels, twin screw. Service speed 15 knots. 358 passengers (168 first-class, 80 second-class, 110 third-class).]

BAD LUCK ∽ German liners had their share of misfortune in the 1930s. The *München* caught fire in New York harbor, at North German Lloyd's Pier 42, at the foot of Morton Street in Greenwich Village. The caption on this Paramount News-Associated Press photo *(above)* read, "The liner *München* seen from the air, flaming at her pier on February 11, 1930. The tremendous clouds of smoke could be seen for miles around. Damage to the ship is estimated at $3 million with two lives lost and eight others injured. Traffic in the Hudson Tubes under the river near this point was cut off for several hours for fear one of the many explosions in the hold of the ship would damage the tunnels." The *München* was later repaired.

48 / THE 1930s: ECONOMICS, POLITICS AND THE EVE OF WAR

DRESDEN ~ During a pleasure cruise to Norway on June 20, 1934, the *Dresden* ran aground near Utsire and was badly damaged. A Norwegian steamer took on the 1,000 passengers and most of the crew, but four remaining crew members perished on the following day when the liner capsized (*opposite, top*). The wreckage was broken up later that summer. The *Dresden* had been launched in 1914 as North German Lloyd's *Zeppelin*, but then sat out the First World War before being seized by the British in 1919. She became the *Ormuz* for the Orient Line and sailed between London and Australia. Her original German owners bought the ship in 1927, renamed her *Dresden* and used her for Bremerhaven–New York sailings and on cruises. [Built by Bremer-Vulkan Shipyard, Vegesack, Germany, 1915. 14,690 gross tons; 570 feet long; 67 feet wide. Steam quadruple expansion engines, twin screw. Service speed 15.5 knots. 971 passengers (399 cabin-class, 288 tourist-class, 284 third-class).]

RELIANCE ~ Perhaps the greatest blow to German passenger shipping in the 1930s was the loss of the renowned cruise liner *Reliance*. The Associated Press in Berlin reported on August 8, 1938, "One member of the crew was killed and several injured in a fire which broke out at Hamburg yesterday in the Hamburg America liner *Reliance*. The fire began at six o'clock in the morning, lasted for hours and taxed firefighting energies to the full. The photo shows clouds of smoke rising from the decks of the blazing *Reliance* and almost obscuring the funnels." (*opposite, bottom*) The ship's gutted remains were cast aside for a time and finally scrapped in 1941.

NIEUW AMSTERDAM (1938) ~ She was the Netherlands's most beloved liner. Originally to have been called *Prinsendam*, she was created during the Depression as a symbol of Dutch resolve. She was also said to be her country's "ship of peace," since no provision had been made in her design and construction for wartime use. Christened on April 10, 1937 by Queen Wilhelmina, she was the largest vessel of any kind yet created in the Netherlands, and even her launching required great skill. Ten large braces had to be fitted to the hull and huge chains attached to these. As the ship was launched, the weight of these chains stopped the new liner from reaching the opposite bank of the narrow River Maas. She was an instant success after entering service, between Rotterdam and New York by way of Boulogne and Southampton, in May 1938. This aerial view (*above*) shows the ship's evening arrival on her maiden voyage. She was a superb blend of Art Deco interiors, Dutch ambiance, and splendid care and service. By the fall of 1939, she was laid up at Holland America's New York terminal at Hoboken, in view of the uncertain political situation in Europe. She was pressed into temporary Caribbean cruise service, but immediately after the Nazi invasion of the Netherlands in May 1940, the Dutch flagship was allocated to the British Ministry of Transport as a troopship. [Built by Rotterdam Dry Dock Company, Rotterdam, Netherlands, 1938. 36,287 gross tons; 758 feet long; 88 feet wide. Steam turbines, twin screw. Service speed 20.5 knots. 1,220 passengers (556 first-class, 455 tourist-class, 209 third-class).]

As a troopship from 1940 until 1945, the gray-painted *Nieuw Amsterdam* carried over 378,000 military passengers on 44 voyages, averaging 8,599 persons per trip. She is shown here, in a photo dated September 12, 1940, departing from her Hoboken berth for Halifax and the beginning of her formal trooping duties *(below)*. Peacetime creature comforts were set aside as the ship's Grand Hall was converted to sleep 600 servicemen, the theater 386 and each former first-class double-bedded room up to 18. With her funnels specially repainted in Holland America colors, the *Nieuw Amsterdam* returned to Rotterdam, her home port, on April 10, 1946, for the first time in over six years *(opposite, top)*. On this highly emotional occasion, a great symbol of liberation and the war's end, she was dubbed the "Darling of the Dutch."

It took fourteen months to gut and refit the *Nieuw Amsterdam* for postwar luxury service *(opposite, bottom)*. "There were plans to re-boiler the *Nieuw Amsterdam* in 1946–47," according to marine artist Stephen Card. "There would have been new uptakes through the dining room and the ship would have had one large funnel, something similar to Cunard's *Caronia*. But the idea was dropped and this later necessitated the re-boilering of the ship twenty or so years later, in 1967."

THE 1930s: ECONOMICS, POLITICS AND THE EVE OF WAR / 51

The *Nieuw Amsterdam* is seen departing from the Wilhelminakade Terminal in Rotterdam in the early 1950s (***above***). The original Holland America offices on the right were converted to a hotel in the late 1990s.

Five Holland America Line ships are seen together in this dramatic aerial view (***opposite***) of the company's Hoboken, New Jersey terminal in 1949. From left to right are the freighters *Blijdendijk* and *Leerdam*; the *Nieuw Amsterdam* in the center; the combination liner *Noordam* and finally the *Arendsdijk*. The area just in front of the *Nieuw Amsterdam* was used as a setting for the 1954 film *On the Waterfront* with Marlon Brando. Several Holland America ships appear as background in the film's sequences.

52 / THE 1930S: ECONOMICS, POLITICS AND THE EVE OF WAR

THE 1930S: ECONOMICS, POLITICS AND THE EVE OF WAR / 53

During the 1960s, as the airlines made deeper inroads into the transatlantic travel market, ships such as the *Nieuw Amsterdam* were used increasingly for single-class tropical cruises. In this view (***below***), Dutch chefs have just put the finishing touches on the so-called "Gala Buffet" in the ship's Grand Hall. It was opened thirty minutes early for photography before the actual serving began.

The *Nieuw Amsterdam* was almost finished in August 1967 when she had a serious mechanical breakdown. There were rumors that the aging ship would be scrapped, but Holland America was fortunate as well as resourceful. Secondhand boilers were bought from a decommissioned US Navy vessel, shipped to Holland and fitted in the liner, which was waiting at the Wilton-Fijenoord shipyard at Schiedam (***opposite, top***). She endured for another six years until December 1973, when soaring fuel costs coupled with her high maintenance made further service impractical. There were rumors that she would become a museum and hotel in Rotterdam harbor, but in reality only scrap merchants were interested in her. She went empty to Kaohsiung, Taiwan, in the winter of 1974 and was later demolished.

WILHELM GUSTLOFF ∼ Kraft durch Freude (KdF [Strength through Joy]) was the section of the Third Reich's national labor organization Deutsche Arbeitsfront (DAF [German Labor Front]). It organized leisure activities on a mass scale for German workers and their families, offering, among other things, inexpensive cruising holidays. This program started in 1934, using passenger ships that had been hard hit by the Depression and might otherwise have been laid up, such as the *Stuttgart*, the *Berlin*, the *Der Deutsche* and some of the Hamburg-South America Line's *Monte* ships. The concept was of single-class cruising, open to all passengers without any form of class distinction or shipboard separation. Many of the passengers on KdF cruises in the late 1930s were in fact country people, unused to the rituals even of domestic travel. One farmer is said to have been told to place his shoes outside his cabin door for polishing; when the steward attempted to carry them off, the farmer slapped him! The success and popularity of these cruises led to the creation of two specially designed liners, the world's first large all-cruise passenger ships. The *Wilhelm Gustloff* (named for an assassinated Nazi official) came first and was commissioned in the spring of 1938. Owned by the DAF, she was managed by the Hamburg-South America Line. Launched by Adolf Hitler, she made news as a floating polling station on April 10, 1938, the day of the plebiscite that ratified the Nazi takeover of Austria. On that day she sailed to Tilbury, in the port of London, took aboard 2,500 Germans and Austrians resident in Britain, who voted on Hitler's plebiscite once the ship left territorial waters, and then returned them to port. She is seen here (***opposite, bottom***) approaching the Tilbury Landing Stage. [Built by Blohm & Voss Shipbuilders, Hamburg, Germany, 1938. 25,484 gross tons; 684 feet long; 77 feet wide. M.A.N. diesels, twin screw. Service speed 15.5 knots. 1,465 tourist-class passengers.]

THE 1930s: ECONOMICS, POLITICS AND THE EVE OF WAR / 55

56 / THE 1930S: ECONOMICS, POLITICS AND THE EVE OF WAR

The *Gustloff*, writes German maritime historian Hans Georg Praeger, "became the pacesetter for construction of special cruising ships." All passengers had outside cabins, thanks to a new type of cabin arrangement. "A larger, four-bedded inner cabin surrounded a smaller two-bed outer cabin and was connected by a light passage with the outer wall and the porthole. Incidentally, the *Wilhelm Gustloff* was the world's first sea-going ship on which, according to instructions, the crew had to be accommodated in exactly the same manner as the passengers." The KdF insisted on ample space for deck chairs and sports and games as well as large, bright halls—as seen here (*opposite, top*)—"with seating accommodation for every holidaymaker and without having to use the dining halls for this purpose." The *Gustloff* and her near-sister, the *Robert Ley*, also had sophisticated fire-safety systems as well as large searchlights, which were fitted to the foremasts and mostly used to light the coastline at night for the enjoyment of the passengers.

ROBERT LEY Slightly larger, but looking similar to the *Wilhelm Gustloff*, the *Robert Ley* followed in the spring of 1939. She was managed by Hamburg America for the DAF. Both ships were purely passenger carriers and were comparatively slow, making only 15.5 knots maximum. The *Ley* (left) is seen here with the *Gustloff* in Hamburg harbor (*opposite, middle*).

Both were victims of the war, destroyed in the final days of conflict in early 1945. The *Gustloff* was torpedoed and capsized while evacuating Germans from Poland. Her loss ranks as the worst maritime tragedy in history: some 5,200 refugees, prisoners, wounded soldiers and crew members were lost. The actual figure, vague because of the lack of official records or passenger lists, may be as high as 5,400. This horrific event had been the subject of several German books and films, but was not brought to the full attention of Americans until a television documentary in 1998. The *Ley* was bombed during the Allied air raids on Hamburg in March 1945. [Built by Howaldtswerke Shipyard, Hamburg, Germany, 1939. 27,288 gross tons; 669 feet long; 78 feet wide. Diesel-electric, twin screw. Service speed 15 knots. 1,774 tourist-class passengers.]

OCEANA Another well known KdF cruise ship was the *Oceana* (*opposite, bottom*), chartered from Hamburg America in the late 1930s. She had been North German Lloyd's *Sierra Salvada*, built for the emigration traffic from Bremerhaven to South America. Seized by Brazil during the World War I and renamed *Avare*, she became the German cruise ship *Peer Gynt* in 1922 and later had a brief stint with the Italian Sitmar Line as the *Neptunia*. Laid up during the war, she was seized by the British in 1945 and was to become the *Empire Tarne*, but instead was sent to the Soviets to become the *Sibir*. She had suffered mine damage and needed a lengthy refit before entering the Soviet Far East service between Vladivostok and the Kamchatka Peninsula. She was broken up at Vladivostok in 1963. [Built by Bremer Vulkan Shipyard, Vegesack, Germany, 1912. 8,227 gross tons as built; 439 feet long; 56 feet wide. Steam triple expansion engines, twin screw. Service speed 13.5 knots. 1,650 passengers as built (120 first-class, 80 second-class, 1,450 steerage).]

VATERLAND Before World War II, Hamburg America planned to replace the four ships of the *Albert Ballin* class with three large liners, according to Arnold Kludas. "The first was the *Vaterland*, but the second and third ships were never named or ordered. Simultaneously, North German Lloyd felt that the *Bremen* and *Europa* would be past their best by 1945, when they would have reached their fifteenth year of service. NGL planned the 80,000-ton *Viktoria*, the first of a pair, for 1942–43." In the event, the *Vaterland* was the only one actually started. She was launched on August 24, 1940, but left incomplete. This model (*above*) shows how the finished ship was to have looked. Her unfinished hull was caught in an Allied air raid on Hamburg in July 1943 and burned beyond repair. Her remains were taken by local scrappers in 1948. [Built by Blohm & Voss Shipbuilders, Hamburg, Germany, 1940. 41,000 gross tons; 824 feet long; 98 feet wide. Turbo-electric, twin screw. Service speed 23.5 knots. 1,322 passengers (354 first-class, 435 tourist-class, 533 third-class).

58 / The 1930s: Economics, Politics and the Eve of War

NOORDAM (1938) ∾ "When the combination passenger-cargo liner *Noordam* [seen here passing the breakwater at Dover, England] and her twin sister, the *Zaandam*, were introduced on the North Atlantic in 1938–39, they caused a sensation," reports Cornelius van Herk, a former Holland America Line master. "They offered high-standard, all-first-class travel only. The accommodations were excellent and the atmosphere intimate. They appealed to a wealthy older clientele, who wanted a quiet sea voyage. There was very little entertainment. A highlight of the day might be some classical records in the lounge after dinner." The *Zaandam* was torpedoed off Brazil in November 1942; the *Noordam* (*opposite, top*), following duties with the Americans during the war, was recommissioned in the summer of 1946. Running nine-day direct sailings between Rotterdam and New York, she was teamed with a slightly larger near-sister, the *Westerdam*. One of them sailed from each direction every other week, usually on Saturdays. [Built by P. Smit, Jr. Shipbuilding, Rotterdam, Netherlands, 1938. 10,726 gross tons; 501 feet long; 64 feet wide. Burmeister & Wain type diesels, twin screw. Service speed 17 knots. 148 first-class passengers.]

The dining room aboard the *Noordam* (*opposite, bottom*) afforded a pleasant, cozy setting. The ship's overall decor was linked to the Art Deco style of Holland America's flagship, the illustrious *Nieuw Amsterdam*, also commissioned in 1938. The *Noordam* and the *Westerdam* also relied heavily on freight. To New York, they carried large quantities of tulip bulbs, wines, seeds, cheeses, agricultural products, and Heineken beer. Homeward, they took such cargo as tin plate, grain, machinery, and meats.

WESTERDAM (1940–46) ∾ The *Westerdam* (*above*) was an especially heroic ship. She survived the Second World War after being sunk no fewer than three times. The *Westerdam* and her sister, the *Zuiderdam*, were ordered in 1939 for Holland America's extended service to the North American Pacific Coast from Northern Europe via the Caribbean and Panama. Soon after construction on the *Westerdam* began, the war started; work continued even after the Germans occupied the Netherlands in May 1940. She was launched in July 1940, but with no important company officials in attendance. A month later, she was sunk during Allied air raids on Schiedam. At the Nazis' order, the ship was salvaged, and construction continued, but at a sluggish pace. The Dutch Underground sank her again in September 1944 when it was discovered that the Germans planned to sink her to block the harbor at Schiedam. The Germans were furious and had the ship raised. The Dutch Resistance soon sank her for the third time. She was salvaged in September 1945 and ready for Atlantic service by June 1946. The proposed *Zuiderdam* was less fortunate. She was sunk in August 1941, salvaged and then sunk again in September 1944. Salvaged after the war, her remains were beyond economic repair and were sent to the breakers in 1948. The *Westerdam* herself was not scrapped until the winter of 1965, at Alicante, Spain; the *Noordam*, sold off in 1963 and later chartered to a French shipper, Messageries Maritimes, as the *Oceanien*, ended her days in a Yugoslav scrap yard at Split in 1967. [Built by Wilton-Fijenoord Shipyard, Schiedam, Netherlands, 1940–46. 12,149 gross tons; 516 feet long; 66 feet wide. M.A.N. type diesels, twin screw. Service speed 16 knots. 134 first-class passengers.]

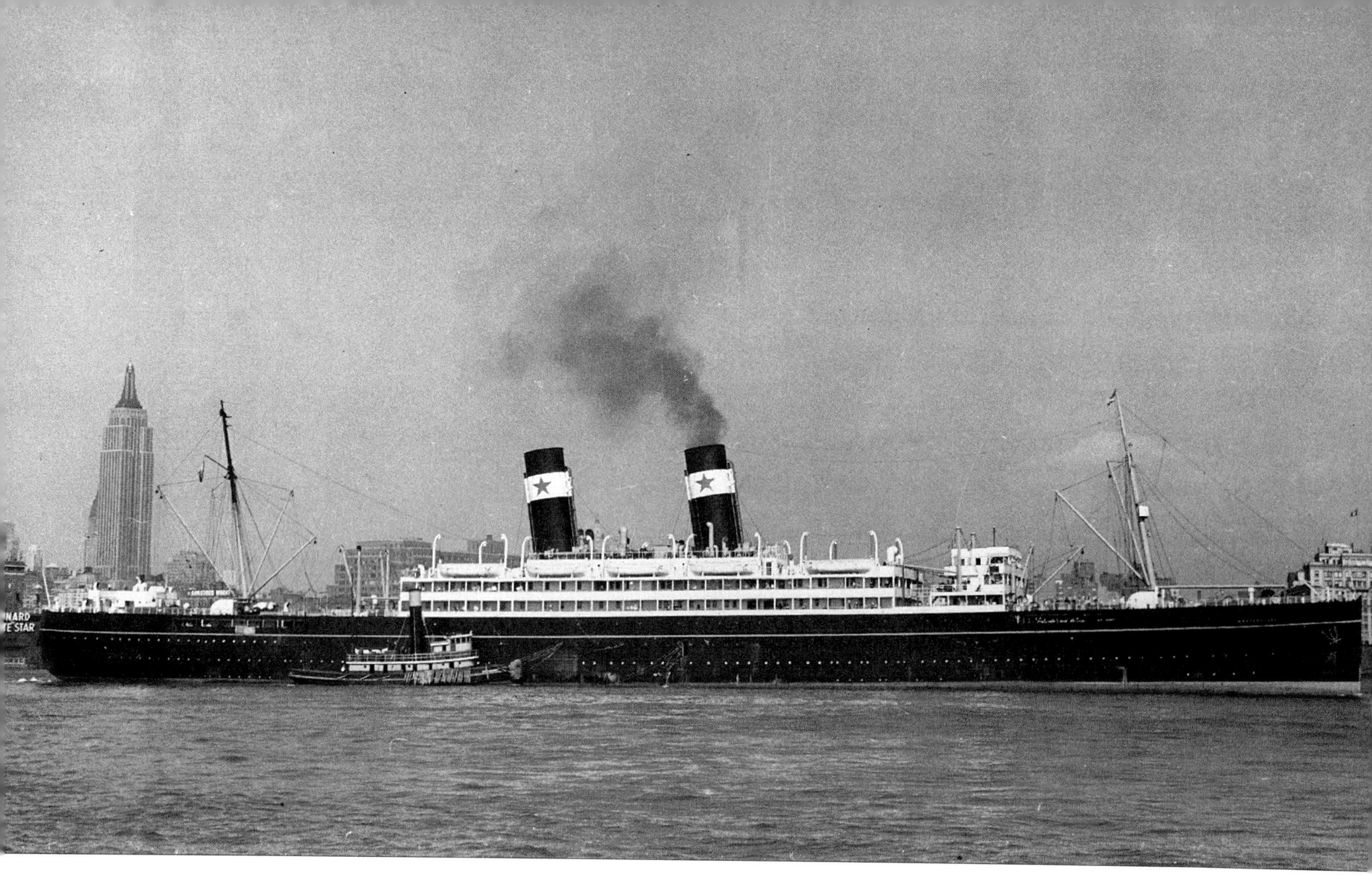

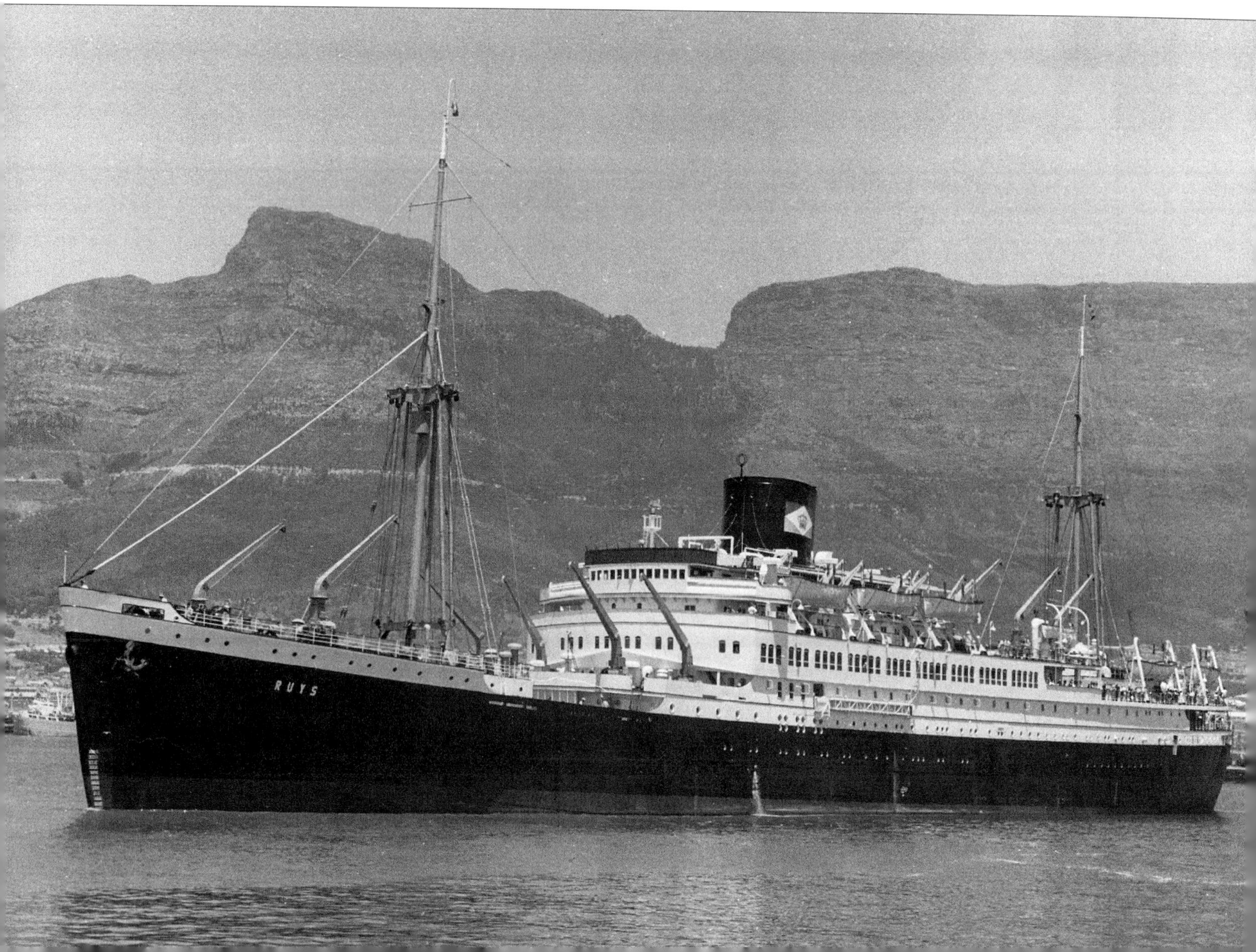
RUYS

WESTERNLAND ∞ The Red Star Line sisters *Westernland*, seen here in the Hudson River at New York *(opposite, top)*, and *Pennland* sailed under the British flag until 1935 when they were transferred to German registry. In the early 1930s, they had been losing money and faced a bleak future on the Atlantic. Red Star was facing collapse. A scheme developed in 1934–35 to make them over as the "lowest priced" ships on the North Atlantic, a concept that included ideas like cafeteria-style dining. However, the British government refused to approve of such an operation and the two ships were sold to Hamburg-based shipowner Arnold Bernstein. He continued to operate them between Antwerp and New York under the Red Star Line banner, but soon faced other troubles. As the Nazis consolidated their control, Bernstein, a Jew, was stripped of his holdings. In 1939, in the final spring before the war, the two confiscated liners were sold to the Holland America Line and placed under the Dutch flag; both soon became troopships for the British. The *Westernland* briefly served, in May 1940, as the seat of the Dutch government in exile while anchored off Falmouth, England. She was sold after the war, in 1946, to be converted to a whaling ship, but the idea was later abandoned and the ship scrapped. The *Pennland* was bombed and sunk by the Germans in Greek waters in April 1941. [Built by Harland & Wolff Limited, Belfast, Ireland, 1918. 16,314 gross tons; 601 feet long; 67 feet wide. Steam triple expansion engines, triple screw. Service speed 21 knots. 2,455 passengers as built (631 cabin-class, 1,824 third-class).]

RUYS ∞ Holland's KPM Line built three combination liners just before the Second World War started, and they were used on an extended service among South Africa, the Dutch East Indies and ports in the Far East as far north as Japan. They were named, for company directors, the *Boissevain*, the *Ruys*, shown here in the 1960s at Capetown *(opposite, bottom)*, and the *Tegelberg*. After the War, KPM merged with another Dutch firm, the Java-China-Japan Line, to form Royal Interocean Lines, a company that almost never sailed to the Netherlands. The *Ruys*, her sisters and several fleetmates were assigned to one of the most extensive passenger ship services of the 1950s and 60s. Each voyage took three months, from Yokohama and Kobe to Hong Kong, Singapore, Port Swettenham, Penang, Mauritius, Lourenço Marques, Durban, and Capetown, and then across the South Atlantic to Rio de Janeiro, Santos, Montevideo, and Buenos Aires. These ships carried all sorts of passengers: old colonials and rich tourists, Chinese and Indian emigrants, even seasonal farm-workers. These three ships, noted not only for high-standard first-class passenger quarters, but for being some of the largest triple-screw passenger ships ever built, lasted until 1968. They were sold for some $500,000 each to Taiwanese scrap metal firms. A crew of six delivered each of them. [Built by De Schelde Shipyard, Flushing, Netherlands, 1937. 14,304 gross tons; 559 feet long; 72 feet wide. Sulzer diesels, triple screw. 386 passengers in three classes.]

ORANJE ∞ When the Dutch shipping firms slowly began to emerge from the leanest years of the Depression, they looked to build their largest and grandest liners yet. For the North Atlantic run to New York, Holland America built the illustrious *Nieuw Amsterdam* of 1938. Two rivals in the East Indies colonial trade, the Nederland Line and Rotterdam Lloyd, also wanted new flagships. Nederland's came first, the *Oranje (above)*, launched in September 1938 by Queen Wilhelmina. A unique ship for her time, she had a single mast and a single stack, and quite contemporary interiors. The colonial connection was not overlooked, however. In first class, the Cane Lounge was done with rattan chairs, exotic potted plants and overhead fans. She had barely entered service in the summer of 1939 when the war started, and she was soon sailing as a hospital ship for the Royal Australian Navy. She survived the war years, resumed her colonial sailings and later sailed regularly on three-month trips around the world. [Built by Netherlands Shipbuilding Company, Amsterdam, Netherlands, 1939. 20,017 gross tons; 656 feet long; 83 feet wide. Sulzer diesels, triple screw. Service speed 21 knots. 717 passengers in four classes.]

THE 1930S: ECONOMICS, POLITICS AND THE EVE OF WAR / 61

On January 5, 1953, while in the Red Sea, the *Oranje* and her greatest rival, the *Willem Ruys* of Royal Rotterdam Lloyd, decided to sail by one another at close range for the entertainment of their passengers and crews. But there was a miscalculation and the two liners collided. Damaged on her starboard side, the *Willem Ruys* had temporary repairs made at Port Said before heading home to Rotterdam. The *Oranje* had bow damage, but continued onward to Jakarta. She is seen here returning to Amsterdam for repairs a month later (**above**). The *Oranje* was sold to the Italian firm Flotta Lauro in 1964 and rebuilt as its *Angelina Lauro*. Later used as a cruise ship, she burned at her berth at St. Thomas in the US Virgin Islands in March 1979. Beyond repair, she was sold to Taiwanese scrappers. On September 23, while en route empty and under tow, she sank in the Pacific. Two weeks later, another empty, scrapyard-bound former liner sank in the Pacific as well: the *Bonaire Star*, formerly the Israeli *Jerusalem* of 1957.

CHAPTER THREE

The 1940s: War, Destruction and Decline

Over a dozen cruise ships participated in commemorative cruises to the beaches of Normandy in June 1994, the 50th anniversary of the invasion of Normandy, the beginning of the end of World War II in Europe. Many great liners had been among the hundreds of ships used to land the invading forces. But the occasion also brought to mind the sad losses of those grim wartime years.

The first sinking by the Nazis was of an unarmed Atlantic liner. She was the 13,000-ton *Athenia*, owned by Britain's Donaldson Line, headed westward on an otherwise normal voyage from Glasgow to Montreal. She was torpedoed and sunk on September 3, 1939, only two days after war was officially declared between the British and the Germans. There were 113 casualties among her passengers and crew. The news was horrifying, the act a breach of every treaty. Publicly, the Nazis denied responsibility. In response, liners were quickly painted over in grays and blacks and darkened by night. Some were even armed with small, mounted guns. But in a matter of weeks others would be lost as well, including Norwegian America's new flagship, the *Oslofjord*. The speedy *Bremen* and the magnificent *Normandie* were destroyed, meeting fiery ends at their berths. The German champion was sabotaged by an unhappy crew member at Bremerhaven while the French Line's flagship was the victim of workers' carelessness at New York's Pier 88.

While the first winter of the war was deeply troubling, the loss of a Cunard liner, the *Lancastria*, was especially horrific. During the hurried evacuation of western France in June 1940, she was attacked by Nazi bombers off St.-Nazaire. Heavily overloaded with passengers, including many British soldiers, she took four hits including one bomb down her smokestack, and sank within twenty minutes. Estimates of the number of people on board range from 6,000 to 9,000; 2,500 survived. Feared as demoralizing to the Allied war effort, news of this disaster was officially withheld for some time (the British government report on the incident is legally suppressed until 2040, for unknown reasons). Months later, in October, there was another crushing blow to the Allies. One of Britain's largest and finest liners, the 42,000-ton *Empress of Britain*, was sunk by a U-boat off Ireland. She was the largest Allied merchant vessel to be sunk during the entire conflict.

Dozens of other liners were sunk, especially at the height of the war in 1942–43. The Dutch lost the *Statendam*, *Dempo*, *Baloeran*, and *Marnix van St Aldegonde*, among others. But the Allies were retaliating as well. Soon Italy's finest luxury ships were destroyed. British bombers attacked and sank the fabulous *Rex*, Mussolini's Atlantic flagship and Italy's only Blue Ribbon holder. Her burnt-out wreckage was cut up after the war ended. In fact, all but four of Italy's liners were lost by 1945, as were all but one ship of the Japanese passenger fleet.

Most of Germany's once huge passenger fleet was shattered in the final months of the war, the fateful winter and spring of 1945. No fewer than fourteen of its large liners were lost between August 1944 and May 1945. The end for the former Nazi workers' cruise ship *Wilhelm Gustloff* was by far the most horrendous. On January 30, 1945, in the icy waters of the Baltic, she was torpedoed by the advancing Soviets. Hideously overloaded, her loss ranks as the worst in all of maritime history: as many as 5,400 refugees, soldiers, guards, crew, and wounded. This disaster is still the subject of books, magazine articles, and television documentaries. Two weeks later, the *Steuben*, another former liner, also went down in the Baltic, killing some 3,000 people. In early May, just days before the German surrender (and therefore liberation of prisoners), the *Cap Arcona*, the prewar luxury queen of the Hamburg-South America Line, was bombed and capsized, claiming another 5,000 lives. Many of them had been concentration camp prisoners. But even after the war was over, there was additional destruction. As late as 1950, a little Holland America Line combination passenger-cargo ship, the 50-passenger *Delftdyk*, struck a live mine in the North Sea. Badly damaged, she had to be completely rebuilt.

The war ensured that German lines such as Hamburg America and North German Lloyd would be out of the passenger ship business for many years. Companies like the German-Africa and Hamburg-South America Lines would never again have an interest in luxury liners. The Dutch lines reawakened slowly. Holland America did not, for example, build another Atlantic liner until 1951, while the old colonial firms that had once sailed to the Dutch East Indies (now Indonesia) were already in slow but steady decline.

On a car trip around the port of Bremerhaven in the summer of 1982, Arnold Kludas pointed out to me the last sunken remains of the liner *Bremen*. Following her fire in 1941 and after being scrapped almost entirely, the double bottom was towed along the Weser and deliberately sunk in the mud upstream from Bremerhaven. The pieces were a curiosity and, in the mid-1990s, another friend, German marine artist Dietmar Borchert, decided to launch a search for what he called "the *Bremen*'s bones." He wanted to retrieve a small piece of the old steel for the maritime museum at Bremerhaven.

Borchert eventually found the wreckage across the river from Nordenham, "among tall reeds and in shallow water," as marine reporter James Shaw noted. "During the low tide you can see the *Bremen*'s remains from the shore," says Borchert. "There is a wreckage buoy attached to it. If you are not afraid of barbed wire fences on top of the Weser Dykes, you can get within 300 meters of the wreckage." In October 1996, with the help with many interested friends and the services of a local diving firm, Borchert succeeded. A section of the hull plate was cut free and today a "bone" of the *Bremen* resides in that Bremerhaven museum.

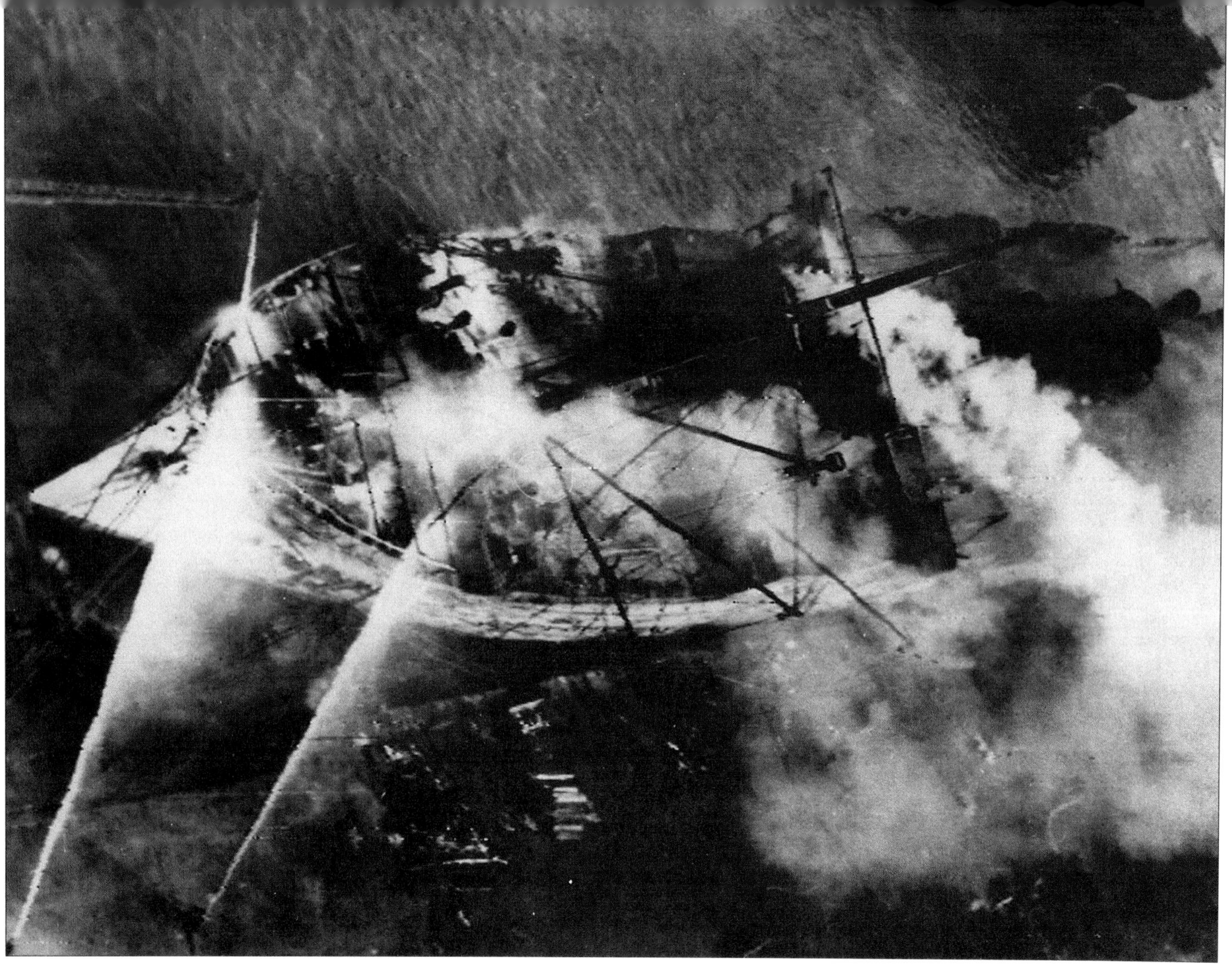

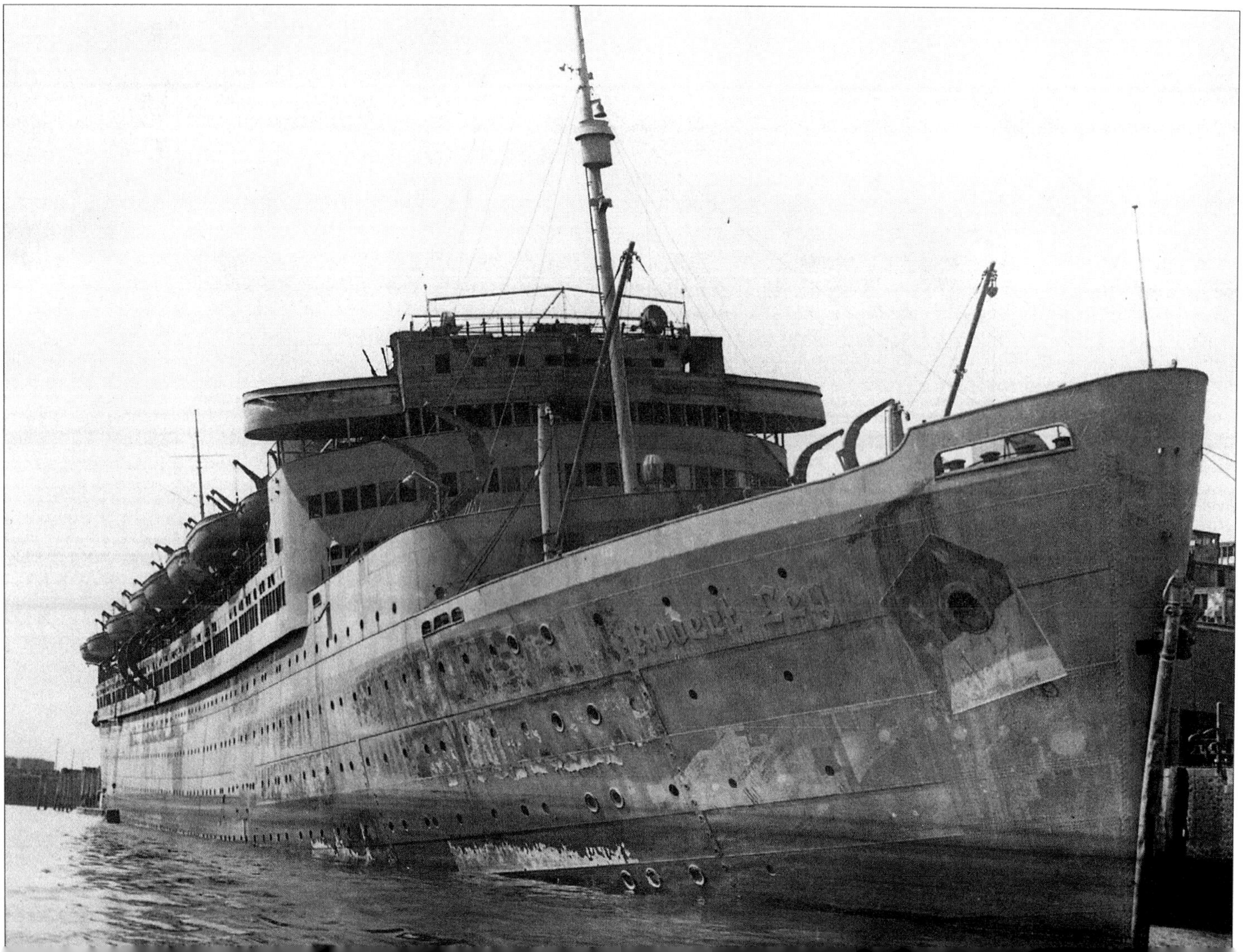

Other Remains of the German Liner Fleet. The former Hamburg America liner *Milwaukee* was seized by British forces in May 1945 and soon became the troopship *Empire Waveney*. Her management was entrusted to one of the Atlantic's great shipping companies, Cunard-White Star. But her days under the British flag were brief. On March 1, 1946, while being refitted at Liverpool, she caught fire and burned beyond repair (*opposite, top*). The hulk was towed to Glasgow for scrapping in January 1947, and the final remains finished off in Troon, also in Scotland, that September.

In a series of photos dated July 30, 1945 showing the bomb-scarred docks of Hamburg, the burnt-out remains of the former KdF cruise ship *Robert Ley* appear (*opposite, bottom*). She had been bombed during the Allied air raids on Hamburg just four months before, in March, and abandoned. There were reports in 1945–46 that she would be repaired and surrendered to the Soviets for use as a passenger ship named *Josif Stalin*, but this never came to pass. Her remains were towed to Britain in 1947 and scrapped.

NEW YORK ~ Once a proud and popular member of the Hamburg America quartet on the Hamburg-New York service, the *New York* spent much of the war as an accommodation ship for the German Navy at Kiel. She made some evacuation runs from Poland, from which the Germans were rapidly retreating in the winter of 1945, but fell victim to Allied aerial attacks on Kiel on April 3. She burned and capsized, and was abandoned (*above*). Her remains were salvaged in March 1949 and soon afterward towed to Britain for scrapping. [Built by Blohm & Voss Shipbuilders, Hamburg, Germany, 1927. 21,455 gross tons; 635 feet long; 72 feet wide. Steam turbines, twin screw. Service speed 15.5 knots. 1,032 passengers (247 first-class, 321 second-class, 464 third-class).]

THE 1940S: WAR, DESTRUCTION AND DECLINE

WILLEM RUYS ~ While the political situation in northern Europe was precarious and even though the East Indian trade had not fully recovered from the Depression, Rotterdam Lloyd felt obliged to build a big liner to complete with the Nederland Line's new, 20,500-ton *Oranje* of 1939. Laid down in January 1939, she was to have been called *Batoer*, and later *Ardjoeno*. Work ceased with the fall of the Netherlands in May 1940, but later the Germans ordered her completed and towed to Germany. Work was slowed deliberately by the Dutch underground, and the Dutch government in exile in London expressly asked that the incomplete ship not be hit in the Allied bombings. Construction resumed in the summer of 1945 and the ship was launched in July 1946, but as the *Willem Ruys*, in honor of the 48-year-old director of Rotterdam Lloyd who had been shot as a Nazi hostage in August 1942. She is seen here in the fitting-out berth at Flushing in an aerial view dated October 6, 1947 (*above*). Running her trials in the fall of 1947, she attained a very impressive speed of 24.6 knots. On her actual delivery date, Queen Wilhelmina granted a "royal" prefix to her owner, which then became Royal Rotterdam Lloyd. [Built by De Schelde Shipyard, Flushing, Netherlands, 1939–47. 21,119 gross tons; 631 feet long; 82 feet wide. Sulzer diesels, twin screw. Service speed 22 knots. 869 passengers as built (344 first-class, 320 second-class, 131 third-class, 74 fourth-class).]

The first-class quarters on the *Willem Ruys* were among the finest on the Netherlands–Indonesia route. The public rooms included the handsome Smoking Salon (*opposite, top*) and the Verandah (*opposite, bottom*).

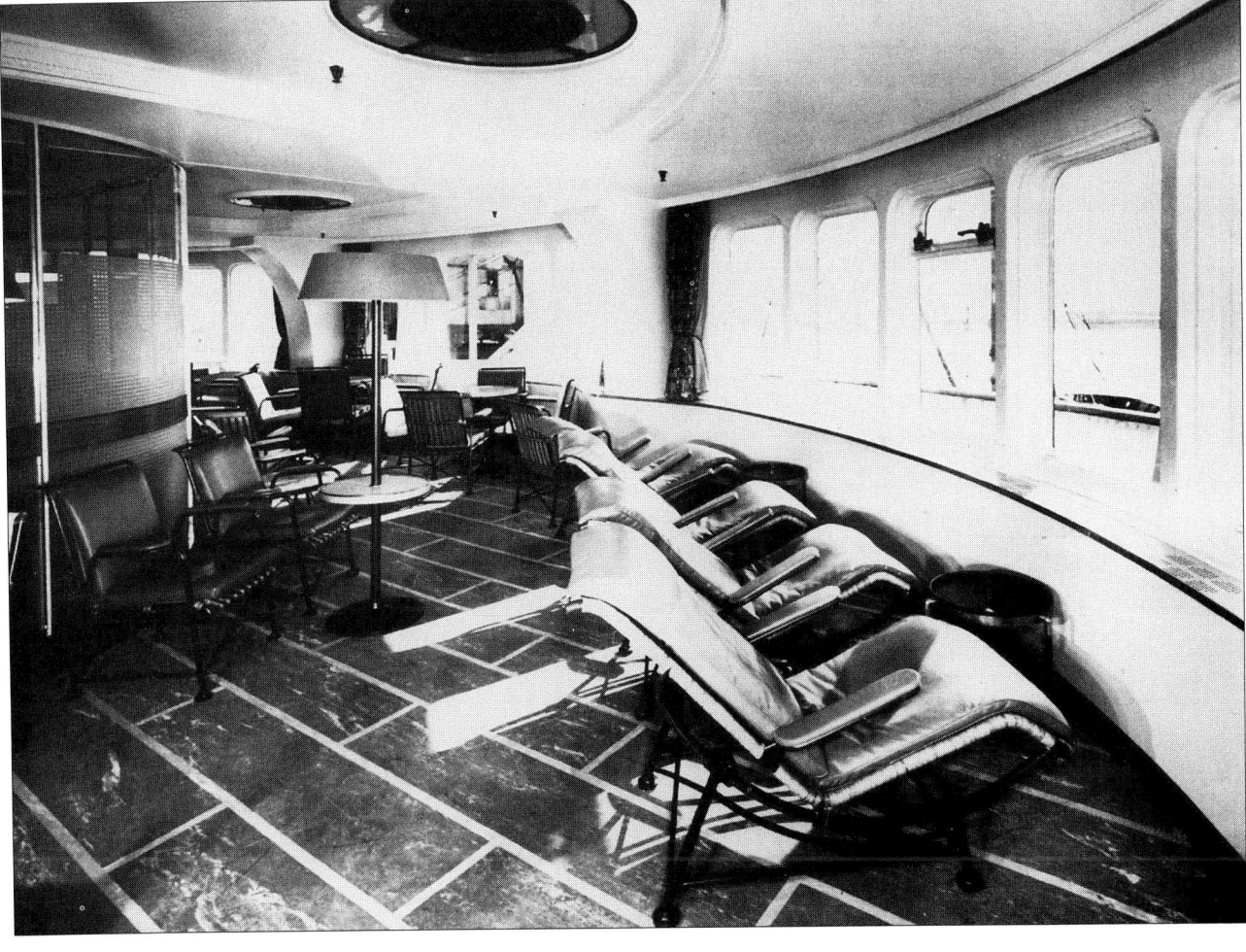

THE 1940s: WAR, DESTRUCTION AND DECLINE / 67

In later years, the twin funnels on the *Willem Ruys* were raised in height, improving her appearance somewhat (*above*). She was sold to the Italian-flag Lauro Line in 1964 and totally rebuilt as its *Achille Lauro* for Europe–Australia sailings and for cruising. In October 1985, she made international headlines when she was hijacked for several days during a cruise in the eastern Mediterranean. Her end came during a sailing from Genoa to South Africa in the fall of 1994. She caught fire on November 30, had to be abandoned, and two days later rolled over and sank off the Somalian coast.

WATERMAN With money short in postwar Europe, but demand for passage, especially at inexpensive fares, increasing, the Dutch decided to convert three American-built Victory-class freighters into passenger ships. They had originally been sold to the Dutch government in 1947 for use as troopships to and from Indonesia, where the Dutch were fighting an anticolonial independence movement. The *Cranston Victory* became the *Zuiderkruis* ("Southern Cross"), the *Costa Rica Victory* the *Groote Beer* ("Great Bear"), and *La Grande Victory* the *Waterman* ("Aquarius"). But by 1951, they were needed in regular, if low-fare, passenger service and were upgraded and refitted. In the decade or so that followed, they carried migrants, troops, workers and, especially on the Atlantic between Rotterdam and Southampton and New York, college students and their teachers or chaperones. The one-way, nine-day passage from New York to Rotterdam was priced at $140 in 1960. Cabins had from three to ten berths and there were also dormitories that slept up to 55. Every cabin contained a wardrobe and at least one or two washbasins. Public lavatories and showers were located on each deck. In this photo, the *Waterman* is seen laid up alongside the *Groote Beer* in 1963 (*opposite, top*). The trio was disbanded by the mid-60s. The *Zuiderkruis* became a moored accommodation ship for the Dutch Navy before being scrapped in 1969, while the other two were sold to Greek interests and were broken up in 1969–70. [Built by Oregon Shipbuilding Corporation, Portland, Oregon, 1945. 9,176 gross tons; 455 feet long; 62 feet wide. Steam turbines, single screw. Service speed 16 knots. 900 one-class passengers.]

SLAMAT Large cargo ships with expanded passenger quarters to meet postwar needs, the *Slamat* (*opposite, middle*) and her sisters and near-sisters, *Mataram, Garoet, Blitar,* and *Langkoeas* usually ran from Rotterdam and other North European ports to the Far East, including Singapore, Hong Kong, and Japanese ports, via Suez. They were designed and ordered in 1939–40, but the war interrupted the project. The ships were re-ordered in 1946. When needed for the Muslim pilgrimage trade, they were certified to carry up to 1,400. Passenger accommodations consisted of a dining room, a lounge, and a portable swimming pool. Their five cargo holds included tanks for the transport of latex and vegetable oils. Later downgraded to pure freighters with only 12 passenger births, they were outmoded entirely by the late 1960s, when new, far larger and faster container ships were taking over the cargo trade. The *Slamat* was sold in 1969 to Singapore-registered Pacific International Lines and, as the *Kota Makmur*, traded around the Far East for nearly a decade. She was sold in 1978 to scrappers in Pakistan. [Built by Rotterdam Dry Dock Company, Rotterdam, Netherlands, 1949. 9,827 gross tons; 515 feet long; 63 feet wide. Sulzer diesels, twin screw. Service speed 16 knots. 35 one-class passengers.]

ALNATI The so-called Rotterdam-South America Line, an arm of the Dutch shipowner Van Nievelt, Goudriaan & Company, ran three combination passenger-cargo liners on the South Atlantic run. These were the *Aldabi, Alhena,* and *Alnati,* shown here (*opposite, bottom*). They were actually built at the beginning of the war, but saw little service for some years. The *Alnati*, built as the *Albiero*, was completed by the Germans and renamed *Wuri*. She was later sunk in the Kattegat, raised and taken to occupied Copenhagen for repairs, only to be sunk once again by the Danish underground. Salvaged after the war, she was sold to Swedes, but then sank for a third time. Rotterdam-South America finally repurchased the ship and had her refitted at Hamburg. She was given high-standard passenger accommodations. There was complete air-conditioning, a portable pool, and a private bathroom for every cabin. Generally, she and her sisters sailed from Rotterdam to Rio de Janeiro, Santos, Montevideo, and Buenos Aires. [Built by Netherlands Dock Company, Amsterdam, Netherlands, 1941. 7,368 gross tons; 477 feet long; 60 feet wide. Stork diesel, single screw. Service speed 13.5 knots. 52 first-class passengers.]

THE 1940s: WAR, DESTRUCTION AND DECLINE / 69

CHAPTER FOUR

The 1950s: Rebirth and Rebuilding

New York harbor was booming in the 1950s. The comings and goings of the ships there seemed hectic and thrilling. Even as an energetic, enthusiastic schoolboy, fascinated by almost everything to do with ships, I couldn't quite take it all in. The big liners came and went with regularity (the Dutch ones usually sailed on Fridays at noon, for example, and the *Bremen* always at midnight) and, at least to me, were much like performers in a long-running soap opera with extended, multifaceted storylines. The liners appeared in varied groupings, since their schedules varied—some appeared weekly, some fortnightly, some every third or fourth week. This was especially true along Luxury Liner Row, those great green piers along the Hudson on Manhattan's West side in the 40s and 50s, where sometimes as many as seven or eight passenger ships at a time were recorded for newspaper centerfolds. Different Cunarders appeared, often one of the big Queens, the *Queen Mary* or the *Queen Elizabeth*, an Italian and a French liner, and inevitably an American, either the *United States* or the *America* and, even more often, the *Independence* or the *Constitution*. Freighters in New York harbor in those days came at an even greater pace. You had only to turn around and there was, say, a United States Lines or United Fruit cargo vessel inbound or one from Grace, American Export or Moore McCormack heading out.

The passenger ship business then was still running at brisk, prosperous levels. Jet airliners, which would by the 1960s replace almost entirely the great worldwide liner services, were not yet an enormous threat; they did not fly the Atlantic until the fall of 1958. Steamship companies remained positive, profitable and optimistic. Among the Dutch and German liners alone, I clearly recall four passenger ships' maiden voyages within two years in the late 50s, each with class-divided transatlantic service. The handsome *Statendam*, as I remember, arrived on a bitterly cold February afternoon in 1957 practically in my backyard, at the 5th Street Pier in Hoboken. Docking it was a long, plodding procedure. It took several hours to nose her into the north side of the terminal because New York harbor tugs were on strike and the sparkling new ship, without a gala reception, had to use her own engines and the guidance of several lifeboats that had been lowered into the chilly waters of the Hudson. The ship was dressed up from end to end; I recall the colorful flags snapping in the winter wind. I remember the summer Friday afternoon in 1958 when the totally rebuilt *Hanseatic* came down the river from Pier 97 on her first outbound sailing. Two slanted funnels, painted in red and black to resemble the French Line's but with vivid white Maltese crosses added, had replaced the three stacks that had marked her earlier days as Canadian Pacific's *Empress of Scotland*. The biggest German liner yet on the Atlantic, she looked smart, proud, impeccable. She too wore extra flags for the occasion. Exactly a year later, in July 1959, on an overcast morning, I stood on the Hoboken shore waiting for another rebuilt German, the *Bremen*.

The sounds of whistles and sirens filled the port as this gleaming new flagship, at reduced speed, majestically made her way up the harbor and along the Hudson. North German Lloyd cleverly exploited the occasion, making sure that the outbound *Berlin* passed the inbound *Bremen* just off the Battery: it was the first time two of its liners had been on the Atlantic since just before the war in the late summer of 1939. Two months later, again at Hoboken, Holland America's innovative and impressive *Rotterdam* first appeared. Immediately after school, I went down to that same pier at the foot of 5th Street. The ship was huge, especially against the Hoboken cityscape. Unusually, the *Rotterdam* had yellow lifeboats. She also had no funnel whatsoever; instead, she had twin uptakes placed aft. She was the first stackless liner on the Atlantic trade. She too was dressed in colorful maiden-voyage flags. Perhaps more than the others, she hinted at the future, with its increasing and rapid changes in ocean liner design.

Overseas, as I learned from the pages of books by Laurence Dunn that I devoured hour after hour, many new passenger ships had come into service during the 1950s. The Dutch, for example, added the *Randfontein* for the African trade and the smart-looking *Oranje Nassau* and her sister for the Caribbean run, while the Germans created six combo sisters for the long service to the Far East. There were also the big refits and makeovers, such as the age-reducing modernization of the *Johan van Oldenbarnevelt* and the upgrading of the *Seven Seas*, which had once been a small aircraft carrier.

Sadly, all this would change in the 1960s. Ships would lose money, be sold, be prematurely scrapped. But at the time the consequences weren't completely clear. The business was changing rapidly, taken over by a new generation of passenger ships designed for leisurely, one-class, amenity-filled cruising. The grand character associated with the great ocean liners disappeared. Midnight sailings and celebratory paper streamers and predeparture *bon voyage* parties would also just about vanish. Even so, however, some of us managed a few trips on some of what we called the "older" liners. I made voyages on at least four ships mentioned in this chapter, the *Hanseatic*, the *Bremen*, the *Rotterdam*, and the former *Maasdam* (as the largely unchanged *Stefan Batory*). They were all wonderful ships, charming and evocative, and have left many memories. I especially recall the gleaming crystal and tableware on the *Bremen* and the shoes placed late at night outside the cabins for polishing. I recall the department-store-like revolving doors on the *Hanseatic* that connected the enclosed promenade with the main foyer, the Japanese lacquer panels and Delft tiles on the *Rotterdam*, and the highly polished veneers and tiny four-passenger elevator on the ex-*Maasdam*. They're all gone now. I sail these days on a new generation of Dutch and German luxury queens built purposely as cruise ships, like the sleek, impeccable new *Maasdam* and the ultraluxurious, art-filled *Deutschland*. We shall never see the likes of those older ships again.

MAASDAM (1952) In the late 1940s, Holland America planned for some new, albeit modest, passenger tonnage: a pair of 60-passenger combination passenger-cargo ships for the long run from northern Europe to the west coast of North America via Panama. They were to be called *Dinteldyk* and *Diemerdyk*. But no sooner had construction begun on the first of them, in December 1949, when Holland America changed its plans. The *Dinteldyk* was redesigned for the quickly reviving transatlantic trade to and from New York as the 861-passenger *Ryndam*. Specifically, she was designed for the less expensive tourist-class trade. Instead of six holds, she was built with seven passenger decks. Soon, the intended *Diemerdyk* was redesigned as well, becoming the *Ryndam*'s sister ship *Maasdam*. A small first class was tucked into what was called the "penthouse" section of the ship. For the first time, tourist class had 90 percent of the accommodations and the greatest range of public areas and amenities. The *Ryndam* entered service in July 1951, the *Maasdam* in August 1952, and together they quickly became extremely popular for their comfortable service and economy—tourist rates began at $20 a day or $180 for the nine-day passage from New York, where the *Maasdam* is shown having just departed from her Hoboken, New Jersey berth (*above*), to Rotterdam. Soon other Atlantic liner companies copied the pair, while Holland America was so pleased that it ordered a larger, more luxurious version, the *Statendam* of 1957. [Built by Wilton-Fijenoord Shipyard, Schiedam, Netherlands, 1952. 15,024 gross tons; 503 feet long; 69 feet wide. Steam turbines, single screw. Service speed 16.5 knots. 861 passengers (39 first-class, 822 tourist-class).]

THE 1950S: REBIRTH AND REBUILDING

The accommodations on the *Maasdam* and her sister were comfortable, varied, and superbly maintained. Here we see the Smoking Room (*above*) on the *Maasdam* as well as the entrance to the tourist-class bar (*right*) and the tourist-class main restaurant (*opposite, top*).

Long popular on the Atlantic run and for their occasional cruises (five days to Bermuda in 1953, for example, were priced from $115), the *Ryndam* and the *Maasdam* began to lose passengers and therefore income by the late 1960s. The *Ryndam* was sold in 1971 and rebuilt as the Greek cruise ship *Atlas*. After 1993, she was moored at Gulfport, Mississippi as a casino. The *Maasdam* became the *Stefan Batory* in 1968 and sailed for the Polish Ocean Line until sold to Greek buyers in 1988. Laid up for much of her final decade, she is seen here (*opposite, bottom*) being demolished at Aliaga, Turkey on May 10, 2000.

THE 1950s: REBIRTH AND REBUILDING / 73

STATENDAM (1957) ~ In every way, the handsome *Statendam*, completed in the winter of 1957, was an improvement on the *Ryndam* and *Maasdam*. On the new ship, for example, some 90 percent of the cabins, regardless of class, had private bathroom facilities. She was faster so that she could run alongside the flagship *Nieuw Amsterdam* and later the new *Rotterdam* as well. And she was more adaptable for off-season cruising, which required, among other features, larger staterooms, more open deck space and a large pool. The ship is seen here *(below)* departing from her Manhattan berth in October 1970. [Built by Wilton-Fijenoord Shipyard, Schiedam, Netherlands, 1957. 24,294 gross tons; 642 feet long; 81 feet wide. Steam turbines, twin screw. Service speed 19 knots. 952 passengers (84 first-class, 868 tourist-class).]

The *Statendam* made news even before she entered service. She was floated out of her construction berth rather than launched in the traditional way, in June 1956. Even her naming ceremony was unusual. On January 23, 1957, during the sea trials, Crown Princess Beatrix poured a glass of champagne over the ship's 300-pound bell, which had been specially positioned in the ship's flower-bedecked restaurant. When the *Statendam* arrived in New York, there was a tugboat strike, so the welcoming festivities were greatly curtailed and the ship was forced to berth herself. Her interiors, such as the tourist-class main lounge *(opposite, top)* and the Ocean Bar *(opposite, bottom)*, were highly praised. As in all Holland America liners, polished wood—in this case bleached ash, Rio rosewood, and African bubinga—featured prominently in the decoration.

74 / THE 1950S: REBIRTH AND REBUILDING

THE 1950S: REBIRTH AND REBUILDING / 75

This first-class room with twin beds, sitting area, and full bathroom (*left*) was priced at $312 per person for a seven-day summer high season sailing between New York and Southampton. The fare was $317 to Le Havre and $322 with the extra day to Rotterdam.

Tourist-class passengers had the greatest share of space on the *Statendam*, including the vast open decks (*below*). Used as a full-time cruise ship beginning in 1966, the ship was sold in 1981 to France's Paquet Cruises and became the *Rhapsody*, and in 1986 became the *Regent Star* for Greece's Regency Cruises. She has been laid up since 1995 when Regency went bankrupt.

76 / THE 1950S: REBIRTH AND REBUILDING

DIEMERDYK ~ After the Second World War, Holland America decided to supplement its Caribbean-Pacific passenger-cargo services with a pair of 60-passenger combination ships. But soon after the keels were laid in 1949, they were redesigned as Atlantic liners with nearly 900 berths each. The proposed *Diemerdyk* became the *Ryndam*, the *Dinteldyk* the *Maasdam*. Shortly afterwards, a slip at the same shipyard was occupied by a third ship, which came off the ways as the *Diemerdyk* (**above**). Plans for a sister were somehow delayed and seven years elapsed before the *Dinteldyk* was completed. [Built by Wilton-Fijenoord Shipyard, Schiedam, Netherlands, 1950. 11,195 gross tons; 494 feet long; 69 feet wide. Stream turbines, twin screw. Service speed 16.5 knots. 61 one-class passengers.]

THE 1950s: REBIRTH AND REBUILDING / 77

78 / THE 1950s: REBIRTH AND REBUILDING

DONGEDYK ⁓ The *Diemerdyk* and her running mates were noted for their high-standard, all-first-class quarters, which included a private bathroom in every cabin. Here we see a cabin with adjoining sitting room (*opposite, top*) aboard the *Dongedyk*. The Caribbean-Pacific route was from Bremen, Hamburg, Antwerp, Rotterdam, and London via Bermuda, Curaçao, and the Panama Canal to Los Angeles, San Francisco, Portland, Seattle, Victoria, and Vancouver. A three-week trip from San Francisco to Rotterdam was priced from $455 in 1957. [Built by Wilton-Fijenoord Shipyard, Schiedam, Netherlands, 1929. 10,942 gross tons; 529 feet long; 65 feet wide. M.A.N. diesels, twin screw. Service speed 16 knots. 52 first-class passengers.]

Voyages from Europe to the Pacific were long and leisurely. When the passenger trade fell away, however, the freight went to bigger, faster container ships. The *Dongedyk* was scrapped in the early 1960s, but the newer *Diemerdyk* and *Dinteldyk* went on to sail for Chinese lines before being broken up in 1979.

TJIWANGI ⁓ In 1949, after a four-year war of independence, Indonesia became a sovereign state. Shortly afterward, two Dutch liners that had been intended for colonial inter-island service were launched. Their owners, Royal Interocean Lines, created a new service for them—from Melbourne, Sydney, and Brisbane to Yokkaichi (a Japanese port near Nagoya)—an 11-day nonstop voyage—Yokohama, Kobe, Keelung, Kaohsiung, and Hong Kong. The *Tjiwangi* (*opposite, bottom*) and her identical sister, the *Tjiluwah*, were popular with Australian tourists who made the full 60-day voyage as a long cruise and who came to call them "big white yachts." The ships also carried interport passengers and cargo: Australian wool to Japan, textiles and manufactured goods from Taiwan and Hong Kong. [Built by van der Giessen Shipyard, Krimpen, Netherlands, 1951. 8,756 gross tons; 479 feet long; 63 feet wide. Werkspor diesels, twin screw. Service speed 16 knots. 222 passengers (104 first-class, 118 tourist-class).]

RANDFONTEIN ⁓ The Holland-Africa Line, an arm of the United Netherlands Steamship Company, ran several combination liners between northern Europe and ports in south and east Africa. The finest, largest, and last of these was the *Randfontein*, which entered service in January 1959 (*above*). Like her predecessors, she too had a large cargo capacity, six holds in all, with freezer space and tanks for the transport of vegetable oils. Her passenger accommodations included a splendid first class in which all cabins had private bathroom facilities, and a very comfortable tourist class. Each class had its own swimming pool and nursery for younger travelers. The *Randfontein* sailed from Hamburg, Antwerp, Amsterdam, and Southampton to Capetown, Port Elizabeth, East London, Durban, and Lourenço Marques. [Built by Wilton-Fijenoord Shipyard, Schiedam, Netherlands, 1958. 13,568 gross tons; 584 feet long; 70 feet wide. M.A.N. diesels, twin screw. Service speed 18 knots. 289 passengers (123 first-class, 166 tourist-class).]

THE 1950s: REBIRTH AND REBUILDING / 79

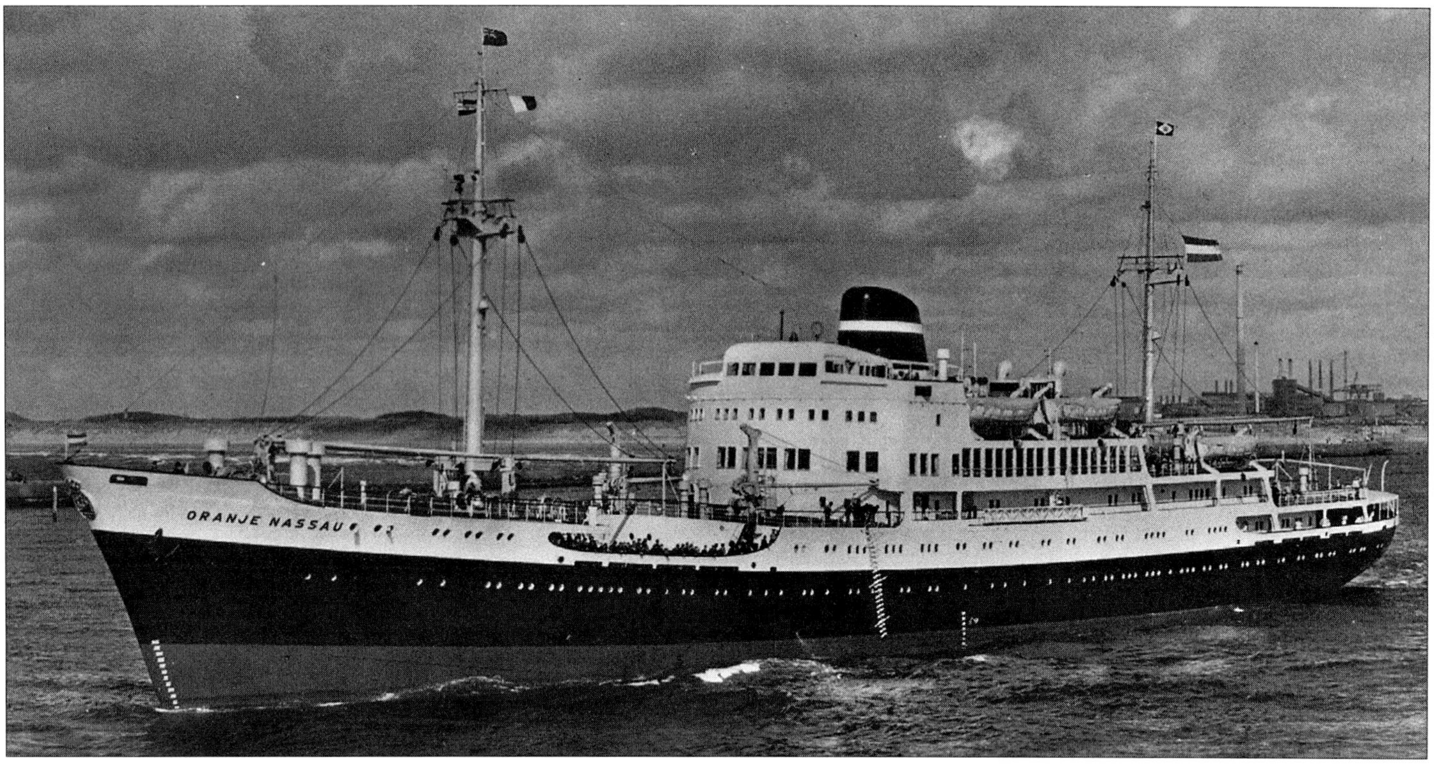
ORANJE NASSAU

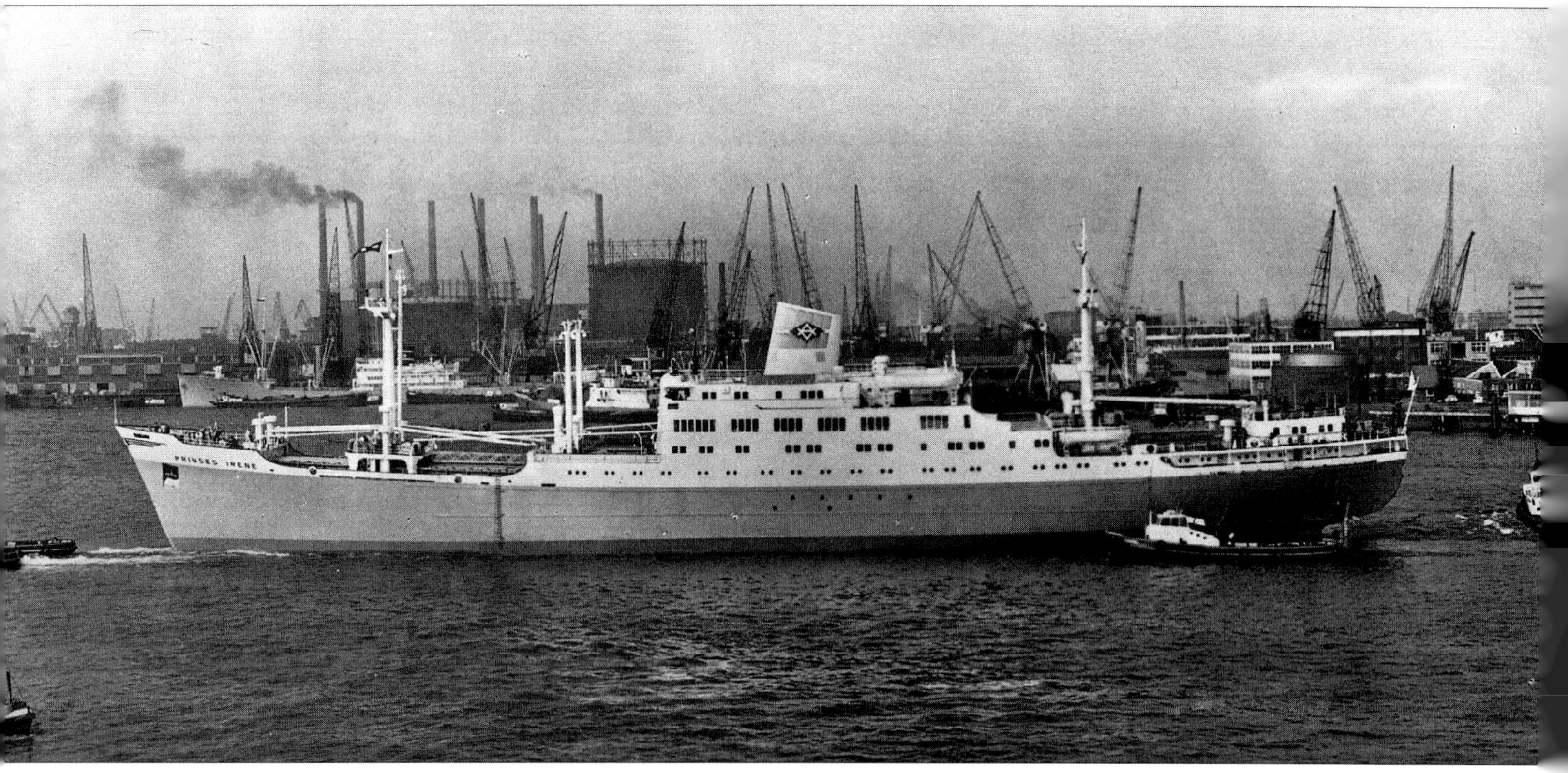
PRINSES IRENE

ORANJE NASSAU ∾ Amsterdam-based Royal Netherlands Steamship Company ran two passenger services from the Netherlands after the war, to the Caribbean and to Surinam in South America. Its fleet, which numbered 60 ships at its peak in the 1950s, was headed by two passenger-cargo liners, the sister ships *Oranje Nassau* (*opposite, top*) and *Prins der Nederlanden*. Superb vessels, they offered a series of public rooms, separate children's facilities including nurseries, as well as dining areas, beauty salons and barber shops, outdoor pools, and partial air conditioning. Many cabins had at least a private shower and toilet. They were used on a 35-day service that took them from Amsterdam and Southampton to Barbados, Trinidad, La Guaira, Curaçao, Aruba, Puerto Limon, Kingston, Santiago de Cuba, and Port-au-Prince. The 17-day trip from Amsterdam to Curaçao cost $500 in the late 1950s. [Built by NV Scheepsbouwerf Gebroeders Pot, Bolnes, Netherlands, 1957. 7,214 gross tons; 432 feet long; 57 feet wide. Stork diesel, single screw. Service speed 15.5 knots. 184 one-class passengers.]

PRINSES IRENE ∾ The Dutch Oranje Line sailed small freighters to eastern Canada and the Great Lakes. Its first passenger ship, the 60-berth *Prins Willem van Oranje*, was added in 1953. But with the opening of the St. Lawrence Seaway in 1959, the company saw opportunities in running a Northern Europe-Great Lakes passenger service. Two high-standard sister ships were built: the *Prinses Irene* (*opposite, bottom*) in 1959 and the slightly different *Prinses Margriet* in 1961. All-first-class ships, they sailed for about eight months of the year from Rotterdam and Southampton to Montreal and Great Lakes ports, terminating at Chicago. In winter, the *Prinses Irene* sailed either to Halifax or St. John, New Brunswick, or to ports in the Gulf of Mexico. Troubled by airline competition, the overall service could not have been less successful. The *Prinses Irene* was soon chartered as a freighter by Cunard and in 1964 was sold to the Indonesian government for use as a military transport; the *Prinses Margriet*, on charter to Holland America for its Rotterdam-New York service, was sold outright to that company. [Built by De Merwede Shipyard, Hardinxveld, Netherlands, 1959. 8,526 gross tons; 456 feet long; 61 feet wide. M.A.N. diesel, single screw. Service speed 16.5 knots. 115 one-class passengers.]

AROSA SUN ∾ A rather unusual passenger vessel for a Dutch line was the accommodation ship *Arosa Sun* (*above*), which housed steelworkers at Ijmuiden from 1960 until sold to Spanish scrappers in 1974. She had a long, rather colorful history. Originally built for France's Messageries Maritimes as the *Felix Roussel*, she traded out of Marseilles on the colonial run to Indochina and had a rather eccentric exterior that included two square stacks. After wartime duties as a British-operated troopship she was rebuilt with a more streamlined single funnel in 1948–50. She was sold to the Swiss-owned Arosa Line, which placed her under the Panamanian flag, renamed her *Arosa Sun* and put her in North Atlantic service to New York and eastern Canada as well as on periodic cruises. But Arosa soon fell on hard times; there were claims against the *Arosa Sun* for as much as $2.3 million in 1959. She was soon seized for debt, and later sold to Dutch owners. [Built by Ateliers et Chantiers de la Loire, St.-Nazaire, France, 1930. 20,126 gross tons; 598 feet long; 68 feet wide. Sulzer diesels, twin screw. Service speed 16.5 knots. 1,049 passengers in 1955 (100 first-class, 949 tourist-class).]

BERLIN (ex-GRIPSHOLM, 1925) ∼ "North German Lloyd wanted to resume their liner services to New York after the Second World War, but had to wait," says Arnold Kludas. "They provided some crew for the passenger ships of the Swiss-owned Arosa Line, which ran passenger service from Bremerhaven to New York and Montreal. But they wanted ships of their own." The Allied restrictions on German companies' owning deep-sea ships was eased very slowly after the war. Larger freighters could be run after 1950 and passenger liners after 1955. North German Lloyd had long wanted to revive its Bremerhaven–New York service and had actually been in partnership with the Swedish American Line for over a year. It ran the *Gripsholm*, under the Swedish flag, for the temporarily created Bremen-America Line on Atlantic crossings out of Bremerhaven. In January 1955 restrictions were lifted, Bremen-America was dissolved, and the ship hoisted German colors and was renamed *Berlin*. Lloyd was back in business. Until the arrival of the new *Bremen* in July 1959, the *Berlin* maintained service singlehandedly. In this view at New York (*below*) dated January 3, 1961, we see her dressed in flags on her return from a two-week Christmas-New Year holiday cruise to the Caribbean, about to dock at Pier 88. In berth from left to right are the *Saturnia*, Italian Line; the *Constitution*, American Export Lines; the *American Scout*, a United States Lines freighter; the *Liberté*, French Line; the *Mauretania*, Cunard Line; the *Ocean Monarch*, Furness-Bermuda Line; the *Sarah Bowater*, a freighter; the *Gripsholm* (a new ship, launched in 1957), Swedish American Line; and finally the *Homeric*, Home Lines. When I visited the *Berlin* on her final sailing from New York, on September 3, 1966, she seemed from another world. She was clearly one of the Atlantic *grandes dames* and retained almost all of her original decor and fittings: heavy, dark woodwork—seen in this view of the first-class smoking room (*opposite, top*)—leather chairs, cage elevator, narrow corridors, and a sense of Nordic heaviness, almost darkness, about her. Afterward, she made a sentimental last cruise from Bremerhaven and then sailed off to Italy to be scrapped. [Built by Sir W. G. Armstrong, Whitworth & Co. Ltd., Newcastle, England, 1925. 18,600 gross tons; 590 feet long; 74 feet wide. Burmeister & Wain diesels, twin screw. Service speed 17 knots. 976 passengers by 1955 (98 first-class, 878 tourist-class).]

ITALIA ∼ The Panamanian-registered *Italia* (*opposite, bottom*), owned by the multinational Home Lines, sailed in the 1950s from Hamburg, Le Havre, and Southampton to Halifax and New York, and later to Quebec City and Montreal. According to Arnold Kludas, "Hamburg America Line, which never returned to transatlantic passenger service after World War II, provided the crews for the *Italia* and another Home Lines ship, the *Homeland*. Hamburg America never had any real plans to return to the New York liner service after the war. By 1946, shares in the company were owned by small freighter and even tugboat companies. They did not think of liners or a revival of New York passenger service." The *Italia* had been the *Kungsholm* of the Swedish American Line, a transatlantic liner as well as a celebrated cruise ship. She was sold to the US government in 1942 and became the troopship USS *John Ericsson* before being sold back to Swedish American in 1947; it promptly sold her to Home Lines. In her final years, beginning in December 1960, she ran weekly, seven-day cruises between New York and Nassau. Minimum fare was then $170. Retired in 1964, she had a short stint as a floating hotel in Freeport, Bahamas before going to Spanish shipbreakers the following year. [Built by Blohm & Voss Shipbuilders, Hamburg, Germany, 1928. 21,532 gross tons; 609 feet long; 78 feet wide. Burmeister & Wain type diesels, twin screw. Service speed 17 knots. 1,319 passengers (213 first-class, 1,106 tourist-class).]

83

84 / THE 1950s: REBIRTH AND REBUILDING

SEVEN SEAS ~ The Dutch lines Holland America and Royal Rotterdam Lloyd decided to capitalize on the reopened German passenger trade and formed the Europe-Canada Line. They took a former emigrant ship, the Panamanian-flag *Nelly*, and reflagged her under German colors. With improvements for transatlantic service, she became the *Seven Seas* in 1953. She is seen here docking at Halifax with the bow of Cunard's *Britannic* in the foreground (***opposite, top***). She sailed from Bremerhaven, Le Havre, and Southampton to Quebec City and Montreal, or to Halifax and New York. In later years, she made educational around-the-world cruises, so-called "floating university" trips. Originally, the *Seven Seas* had been designed as an American freighter, the *Mormacmail* for the Moore McCormack Lines, but was redesigned while still under construction as a small aircraft carrier, a "baby flattop," and completed in 1941 as the USS *Long Island*. Declared surplus and about to be scrapped in 1947, she was bought by Norwegian owners and rebuilt as a low-fare passenger ship. She entered service as the *Nelly*. A mechanical breakdown in the North Atlantic in 1965 spelled her end. She was soon retired and made over as an accommodation ship at Rotterdam. She was scrapped in 1977. [Built by Sun Shipbuilding & Dry Dock Company, Chester, Pennsylvania, 1940. 12,575 gross tons; 492 feet long; 69 feet wide. Sulzer diesels, single screw. Service speed 16.5 knots. 1,007 passengers (20 first-class, 987 tourist-class).]

FRANKFURT ~ According to Arnold Kludas, "When North German Lloyd ordered three 86-passenger combination ships, the *Bayernstein*, *Hessenstein*, and *Schwabenstein*, for the Europe-Far East run in the early 1950s, Hamburg America felt that it had to follow and ordered three almost identical ships of its own. These were the *Frankfurt* (***opposite, bottom***), *Hamburg*, and *Hannover*." The ships were considered so significant to the rebirth of the West German merchant marine that a special stamp was issued in honor of their completion. These ships had extremely high-standard quarters on four decks. Public areas included a main lounge, a reading-writing room, a cocktail bar, an enclosed promenade arranged as a winter garden, a dining room, a beauty salon, and a children's playroom. There was a small pool on deck. All cabins had private bathroom facilities and individual climate control. The ships sailed from Hamburg, Bremen, Antwerp, Rotterdam, and Southampton via Genoa to Port Said, Suez, Aden, Penang, Port Swettenham, Singapore, Miri, Manila, Hong Kong, Yokohama, Nagoya, and Kobe. They also stopped at Colombo and Marseilles on their homeward passages. [Built by Bremer-Vulkan Shipyard, Bremen, West Germany, 1954. 8,959 gross tons; 538 feet long; 64 feet wide. M.A.N. diesel, single screw. Service speed 16.5 knots. 86 first-class passengers.]

The six German Far East ships were among the finest combination liners of their time. The very contemporary accommodations included the verandah cafe (***top***) on the *Bayernstein* and the verandah cafe (***middle***) and the sitting room of a single-bed cabin (***bottom***) on the *Frankfurt*.

THE 1950S: REBIRTH AND REBUILDING / 85

ARIADNE ~ Built for the North Sea trade between London and Gothenburg, the *Patricia*, which also made wintertime Caribbean cruises out of New York, was less than successful for Swedish Lloyd. Hamburg America bought the six-year-old ship in 1957 and upgraded her for longer cruise voyages to Norway, Spitzbergen and the Baltic, the Mediterranean, West Africa, the Caribbean, and South America (including sailings on the Amazon River). Seen here in this 1959 view at New Orleans (*above*), she was again a money-loser. "Hamburg America briefly thought of reviving something of its prewar cruise service and so they bought the little *Patricia* from Sweden," notes Arnold Kludas. "But she was too small, not the right ship. She was unsuccessful and soon sold." Miami-based Eastern Steamship Lines bought her in 1961, kept her enchanting name and ran her, under the Liberian flag, on charter cruises and later from Florida ports. She was sold to Greece's Chandris Cruises in 1972 and sailed as the *Freeport II*, the *Bon Vivant*, and finally as the *Ariane*. She was sold to Cypriot owners in 1989 and renamed *Empress Katerina*, and later found her way to Far Eastern waters where she cruised and served as a floating casino and as a prop in films. She finished up at the scrappers in 1997. [Built by Swan, Hunter & Wigham Richardson Limited, Newcastle, England, 1951. 7,775 gross tons; 454 feet long; 58 feet wide. Steam turbines, single screw. Service speed 18.5 knots. 249 first-class passengers.]

SANTA ISABEL ~ "The famous Hamburg-South America Line never seriously considered re-entering the liner trades to South America after the Second World War," said Arnold Kludas. "They had been bought by Mr. Oetker, a businessman who wanted to be very cautious by the late 1940s. He saw freighters as the future. Besides, the Argentines themselves were building new passenger ships for the Europe-South America run. There was no longer a place for German passenger ships to the South Atlantic." Hamburg-South America did, however, build six passenger-cargo ships with limited passenger accommodations. There were the sisters *Santa Catarina*, *Santa Elena*, *Santa Isabel*, and *Santa Ursula*, and then a final pair, the *Santa Ines* and *Santa Teresa*. The *Santa Isabel* (*opposite, top*) and her sisters were among West Germany's first deep-sea passenger ships to be built after the war. Their passenger quarters, while very comfortable, had only partial air-conditioning (mechanical ventilation in the staterooms themselves) and shared bathroom facilities between cabins. These ships sailed from the traditional North European ports, Hamburg, Bremen, Rotterdam, and Antwerp, to South American east coast ports such as Recife, Salvador, Rio de Janeiro, Santos, Montevideo, and Buenos Aires. [Built by Howaldtswerke Shipyard, Hamburg, West Germany, 1951. 6,982 gross tons; 479 feet long; 61 feet wide. M.A.N.-type diesel, single screw. Service speed 13 knots. 28 first-class passengers.]

The public rooms aboard the *Santa Elena* (*opposite, bottom*), a sister ship to the *Santa Isabel*, had something of a pre-World War II style about them. This was perhaps deliberate, a reminder of grander days of luxury liners such as the *Cap Arcona*.

THE 1950S: REBIRTH AND REBUILDING / 87

HANSEATIC (1930) ~ North German Lloyd was not alone in being interested in reopening German luxury liner service to New York. Several investors joined forces and together with the very successful Home Lines, formed the Hamburg Atlantic Line in 1957. While unable to build a new ship, they bought the *Empress of Scotland*, a well-known three-stacker owned by Canadian Pacific Steamships. She was brought to Hamburg, gutted and rebuilt as the completely modernized *Hanseatic* (*above*) in the summer of 1958. She had been the *Empress of Japan* in the 1930s, sailing between Vancouver and the Far East, and for many years ranked as the fastest liner on the Pacific. She had been renamed *Empress of Scotland* in 1942. As the *Hanseatic*, she divided her time between crossings and cruises. In September 1966, just hours before her departure from New York's Pier 84, fire broke out and engulfed the ship. Repairs were possible, but the smell of smoke had permeated the 36-year-old liner. She was simply too old to repair and so was towed empty across the Atlantic and demolished in the backwaters of Hamburg Harbor. [Built by Fairfield Shipbuilding & Engineering Company, Glasgow, Scotland, 1930. 30,029 gross tons as rebuilt; 672 feet long; 83 feet wide. Steam turbines, twin screw. Service speed 21 knots. 1,252 passengers (85 first-class, 1,167 tourist-class).]

BREMEN (1939) ~ The French liner *Pasteur* had been built just before the start of the Second World War for the Bordeaux–South America trade, but was rushed into service as a troopship. Plans to restore her as a luxury liner in 1946 never came to pass and instead she remained on long-term charter to the French government to carry soldiers, often to and from Indochina, then in revolt. When that work ended by 1956, she was laid up. North German Lloyd, pleased with the success of the *Berlin*, added in 1955, wanted a larger, more luxurious ship, and saw the *Pasteur* as having great potential as its new flagship. Gutted and remade, she entered service as the *Bremen*, surely the most illustrious German ocean liner name, in July 1959. She sailed the traditional route, from Bremerhaven to New York and back via Southampton and Cherbourg. In winter, she headed for the sunny Caribbean, mostly on two-week cruises out of New York, and later also made leisure trips from Bremerhaven to such places as Iceland, Scotland, Norway, and the Canary Islands. The caption on this Associated Press photo, dated February 15, 1964, reads, "A lifeboat leads liner *Bremen* to its berth as she prepares to tie up in New York Harbor Feb. 15. In the absence of tugs on strike, the master of *Bremen* lowered two of his own lifeboats to help steer the vessel into the harbor's 'dead water.'" (*opposite, top*) At the end of her German days, however, her engines proved troublesome and gradually the superbly run North German Lloyd lost interest in her. In late 1971, she was sold to the Greek Chandris Cruises, which renamed her *Regina Magna* and ran her fulltime on cruises to Scandinavia, the Mediterranean, and the Caribbean. Soaring fuel prices ended her sailing days in 1974 and she was later sold to a construction company that used her as an accommodation ship for up to 3,600 workers in Saudi Arabia. She was renamed *Saudi Phil I* and then *Filipinas Saudi I* before being sold to Taiwanese shipbreakers in 1980. She never made that last trip, however. On June 6, 1980, under tow in the Indian Ocean, the empty ex-liner heeled over and sank, her great bow pointing upwards before the final plunge. [Built by Chantiers de l'Atlantique, St.-Nazaire, France, 1939. 32,336 gross tons as rebuilt; 697 feet long; 88 feet wide. Steam turbines, quadruple screw. Service speed 23 knots. 1,122 passengers (216 first-class, 906 tourist-class).]

During her reconstruction in 1958–59, the *Bremen* lost almost all traces of her earlier days as a French passenger ship. This view shows the sitting room of a deluxe first-class stateroom (*opposite, bottom*).

THE 1950s: REBIRTH AND REBUILDING / 89

PIER C
AMERICAN EXPORT LINES
BOKEN-PORT AUTHORITY PIERS
E2
E1
ROTTERDAM
ROTTERDAM
M

ROTTERDAM (1959) ~ While Holland America's *Nieuw Amsterdam* was popular and profitable and probably the most beloved of all Dutch passenger ships, the company needed a new flagship by the 1950s. Thought had been given to building a sister ship just after the war, in the late 1940s, but money was short and the future of Atlantic liner travel uncertain. The sisters *Maasdam* and *Ryndam* of 1951–52 were a great success, but they were smallish, quite slow, and catered primarily for the low-fare tourist trade. A successor, the larger, finer *Statendam* of 1957, sparked the idea of a big, luxurious liner that would be the new Dutch merchant flagship. "The *Rotterdam* was a very special ship," according to artist Stephen Card. "She had a 'soul.' You could feel it." [Built by Rotterdam Dry Dock Company, Rotterdam, Netherlands, 1959. 38,645 gross tons; 748 feet long; 94 feet wide. Steam turbines, twin screw. Service speed 20.5 knots. 1,456 passengers as built (401 first-class, 1,055 tourist-class).]

Queen Juliana did the honors at the naming ceremonies on September 13, 1958, and her daughter, Crown Princess Beatrix, joined the *Rotterdam*'s maiden voyage to New York exactly a year later. The liner is seen here (**left**) arriving at her 5th Street pier in Hoboken for the first time. The ship caused a sensation: she was the first new Atlantic liner to do away with the traditional funnel and instead use twin side-by-side uptakes, and she had the best interchangeable design elements between first and tourist class. Easily convertible for one-class cruising with a club-like 730 guests, she brought new standards of luxury and comfort to the Atlantic liner trade.

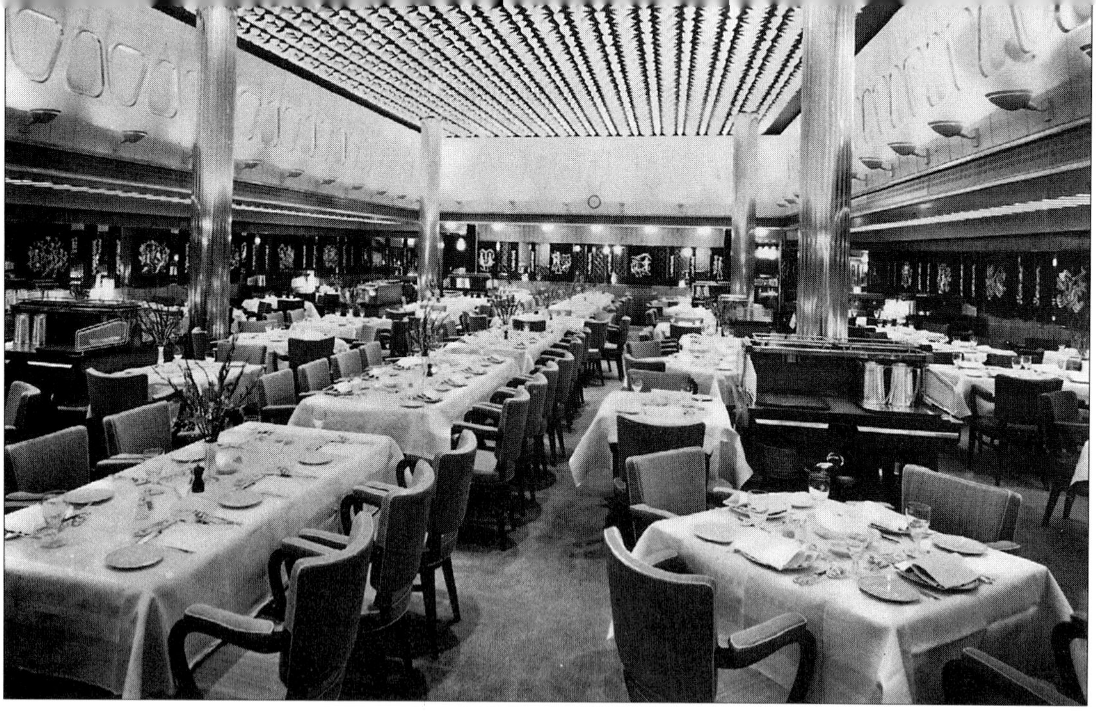

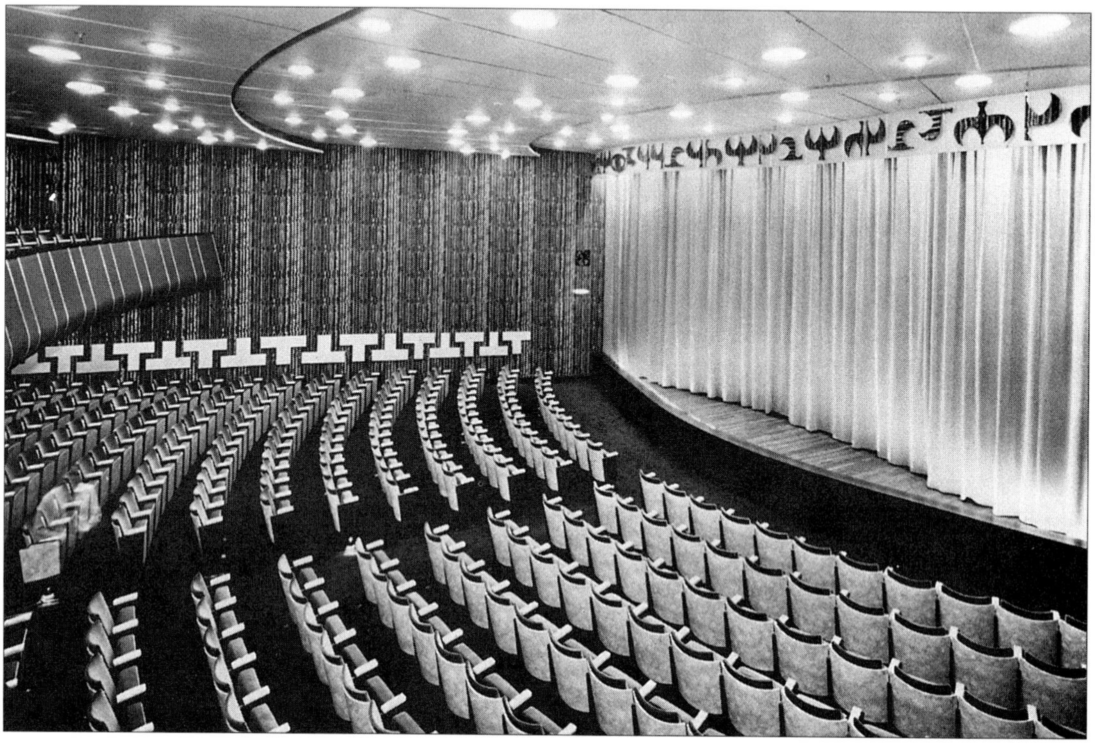

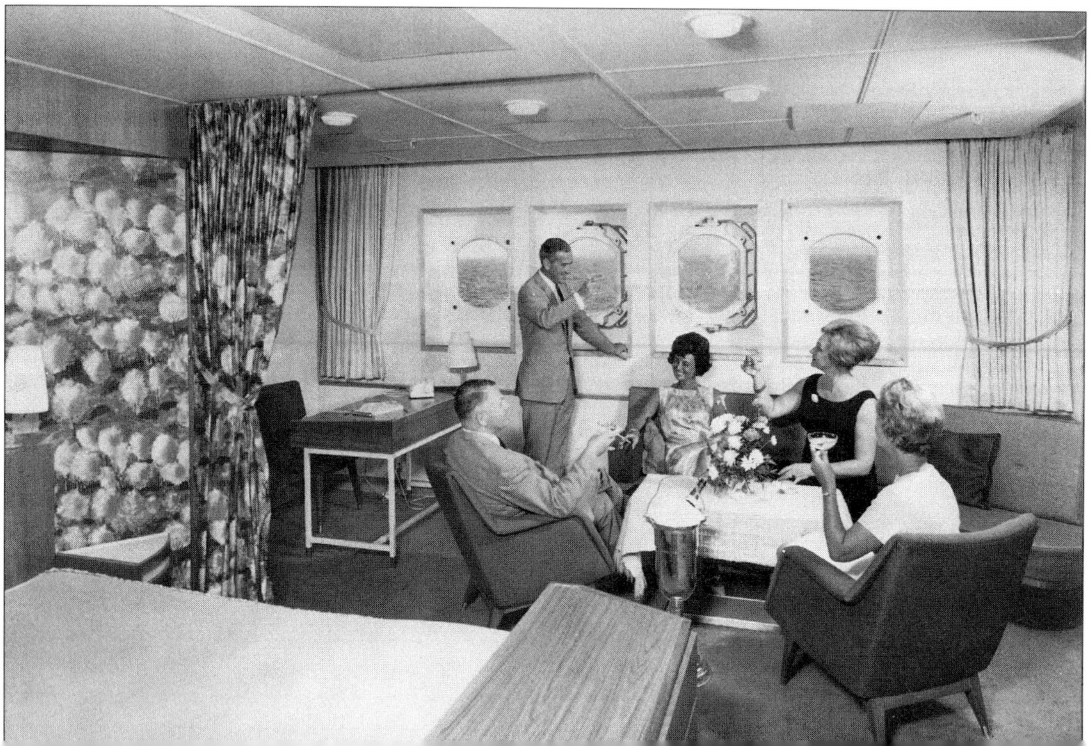

Deservedly, the *Rotterdam* won high praises from passengers soon after her delivery. She was in every way the superb "ship of state." Almost everything about her was characteristically Dutch. On her twelve passenger decks, there were no fewer than fifteen public rooms, and the decoration used fine woods such as Bangkok teak, Japanese ashwood, olive, and French walnut. She was fully air-conditioned, had a shopping arcade, a gym, and indoor and outdoor pools, and had private bathroom facilities in all first-class and most tourist-class cabins. The twin dining rooms, one of which is seen here (*opposite, top*), were connected by a vestibule and together could seat 894 guests. The decor and furnishings of the two rooms were nearly identical, allowing them both to be used when the ship sailed on all-first-class cruises.

The *Rotterdam* could boast of the largest theater then afloat, seating 607 on two levels (*opposite, middle*).

This first class cabin with double bed included a sitting room with four ocean-view windows (*opposite, bottom*). On the ship's first 90-day around-the-world cruise in January 1961, the minimum fare was $1,395; by 1983, it was $15,600; by 1997, $29,900.

Like a number of ships, including the larger *France*, the *Rotterdam* was built too late for a long career on the class-divided Atlantic run. The airlines had 95 percent of the business by the mid-1960s. Within ten years, Holland America had to rethink its plans, and ships such as the *Rotterdam* were made over as full-time cruise liners, running weekly seven-day cruises to Bermuda and Nassau for $200 per person. She is seen here (*above*) in a weekend gathering of cruise ships at New York in June 1977. The Soviet *Kazakhstan* is in the foreground, then the *Rotterdam*, the *Oceanic*, the *Doric* (rather obscured), the *Queen Elizabeth 2*, and (with her funnel just above the *QE2*'s aft decks) another Holland America cruise ship, the *Statendam*.

THE 1950S: REBIRTH AND REBUILDING / 93

The *Rotterdam* became the *grande dame* of cruise ships by the 1990s. Sailing out of Vancouver, she spent her summers in Alaska, where she is seen in Glacier Bay (***below***), and the remainder of the year in the Caribbean or on her annual 90-or-so-day trip around the world. On these gala circumnavigations, some passengers came year after year. Some barely went ashore but preferred to play bridge onboard, while at least one lady flew in her plastic surgeon for a tuneup, recovering during the journey. By 1997, however, the *Rotterdam* was aging, growing troublesome and more costly to operate than Holland America's new generation of sleek cruise ships. Amidst rumors that she would go home to Rotterdam and become a museum, she was sold to struggling Premier Cruises, a multinational firm based in Florida, and renamed *Rembrandt* in honor of her Dutch heritage. Premier was bankrupt by September 2000 and the ex-*Rotterdam* was sent to the Bahamas to await an auction.

CHAPTER FIVE

The 1960s: A Shift in Trades

When 21-year-old Crown Princess Beatrix of the Netherlands arrived in New York on the maiden voyage of the *Rotterdam* in September 1959, she began a round of official duties and engagements in and around Manhattan. Among her stops was an official inspection of Holland America Line's innovative new terminal, then under construction at Pier 40 on the Hudson River at West Houston Street in Greenwich Village. The new pier, costing a then-impressive $18.5 million, would serve Holland America's passenger and freight operations. By 2000, having long been closed to commercial shipping, Pier 40 was part of New York City's Westway redevelopment project. Plans for the huge terminal were still unclear, but ideas included an art museum, a community center, even a rooftop "beach" and swimming pool.

Pier 40 officially opened in March 1963 with a sailing by the *Statendam*. It was closed to deep-sea ships in November 1974 when the Holland America Line moved north to the newly consolidated Passenger Ship Terminal between West 48th and West 52nd streets. Back in the late 1950s and 60s, New York harbor was still booming, not only with passenger liners, but with pre-containerized freighters. Many companies could not even lease prized Manhattan dock space and had to settle for less convenient New Jersey, Brooklyn, or Staten Island. Holland America had long wanted to leave its 5th Street terminal across the Hudson in Hoboken. High taxes and parking problems prompted the company, after some ninety years, to approach New York officials and agree upon a long lease for a new terminal. Four decaying, turn-of-the-century railway piers were removed and in their place went the 805-by-810-foot structure. Uniquely among West Side marine terminals, it could handle three liners at once, or two liners and two smallish freighters. Efficient cargo handling areas included space for no fewer than 125 trucks. Dutch freighters were then landing large consignments of Heineken beer, cheese and, of course, tulip bulbs. Outbound, they sailed to Europe with general freight, including American manufactured goods, heavy machinery, and partially assembled automobiles. Provisions for passengers included lounges, customs and luggage areas, a restaurant, Holland America offices, and perhaps most thoughtfully, rooftop parking for some 1,500 cars. Travelers might depart in January on the *Rotterdam*'s 90-day around-the-world cruise and return in April only minutes away from their cars and the trip home.

In the 1960s, Holland America was still running a busy transatlantic liner service between Rotterdam, Le Havre, and Southampton and New York with such ships as the 1938 *Nieuw Amsterdam*, the *Maasdam* of 1952, and the *Westerdam* of 1946. In winter, most of these Dutch ships sailed to warmer waters, often on two- and three-week cruises to the Caribbean. Generally, schedules were arranged for noontime departures on Fridays for Europe and often at ten in the evening for cruises. Dutch sailors became familiar to residents of adjacent Greenwich Village and, with two- and three-night layovers then customary for most ships, some even received invitations for dinner. Holland America later arranged subleases to such companies as the Norwegian America Line, the Grace Line, and the German Atlantic Line, and to freighter companies like the Venezuelan Line. Special visitors included transatlantic student ships, other Dutch liners on world cruise voyages, and P&O's mighty *Canberra*. But the 1960s were an era of change. The old transocean liner services were quickly faltering in the face of airline competition. The future of passenger shipping was in cruising. Holland America was down to one ship on its Rotterdam-New York run by the late 60s, the veteran, often struggling *Nieuw Amsterdam*; it gave in completely and turned to full-time cruising by the fall of 1971. The entire passenger industry was rattling with change.

As built, Pier 40 was crowned by a specially made twenty-foot-long model of Holland America's flagship *Rotterdam*. It was removed in 1974, and its whereabouts were long a mystery. In 1991, a retired Holland America official told me that the plan had been to return the model to the Netherlands, but that it had been badly damaged by New York's ever-changing weather. Sadly, it turns out that it was scrapped after being lowered to the West Street curbside. Perhaps when Pier 40 is reopened for some special use, some mention will be made of those bygone days of grand ocean liner travel. Myself, I can almost still hear the thundering steam whistles of the old *Nieuw Amsterdam*.

EUROPA (1953) ~ The Swedish American Line had some of the finest liners afloat, and when its 1953 Dutch-built *Kungsholm* went up for sale in the fall of 1965, North German Lloyd jumped at the chance to buy it. It paid $8.5 million for the superb ship, the first Atlantic liner to have all outside cabins as well as private facilities in all rooms, and with just a few cosmetic changes, made her over as the *Europa (above)*. Used initially on transatlantic crossings, she became a full-time cruise ship and soon had a devoted following, especially among Germans. She had a club-like quality about her that suited her many repeat passengers. After running many cruises from Bremerhaven and Genoa, however, the Lloyd looked to replace this beloved veteran. A new *Europa* was ordered and delivered by 1981, and the old one was sold to Italy's Costa Line, which wanted to use her at least part-time in the German cruise market. She was renamed *Columbus "C"*, in deference to the famed, still well-remembered North German Lloyd liner of the 1920s and 30s. But her new career was rather short. In July 1984, while attempting to dock in high winds at the Spanish port of Cadiz, she rammed the outer breakwater and was badly holed. She made it to her berth and landed her passengers, but then heeled over onto the dock. Later righted, she settled on the harbor bottom. She was subsequently pumped out, towed away, and scrapped. [Built De Schelde Shipyard, Flushing, Netherlands, 1953. 21,141 gross tons; 600 feet long; 77 feet wide. Burmeister & Wain diesels, twin screw. Service speed 19 knots. 802 passengers as built (176 first-class, 626 tourist-class).]

HANSEATIC (1964) ~ Israel's Zim Lines decided to reinforce its Haifa-New York service with a lavish new flagship in 1964, but it was too late. The *Shalom* was never successful. She was hard-hit by airline competition, sailed single-handedly and therefore had great voids in her schedule, and was less than popular because of her Kosher standards. Within three years, by the late summer of 1967, she was for sale. The Hamburg Atlantic Line, which had lost its *Hanseatic* to a fire in September 1966, was anxious to restart service, on both Atlantic crossings and cruises. It restyled itself the German-Atlantic Line and bought the *Shalom*, which it renamed *Hanseatic (below)*. It was very optimistic and planned a large companion ship as well, the *Hamburg*, due in the spring of 1969. But while the *Hanseatic* made some two-class crossings, her future was in cruising. She made longer trips on occasion, including voyages of 57 days around South America and 60 days to the Mediterranean, from Port Everglades, Florida. But when fuel prices skyrocketed from $35 to $95 a ton in 1973, German Atlantic fell on hard financial times. The *Hanseatic* was soon sold, going to Home Lines and becoming its *Doric*, used mostly for seasonal New York–Bermuda service. She was sold again in 1981, to Royal Cruise Lines, which sailed her as the *Royal Odyssey* on worldwide itineraries. Another sale followed in 1988 when she became the *Regent Sun* for Regency Cruises. After Regency collapsed in October 1995, the *Sun*, as she was renamed by the banks that held her mortgages, was sent to Florida and then to the Bahamas to await auction. Rumors about her future were frequent. At one point, she was to become the *Michelangelo* for Premier Cruise Lines and later to be rebuilt as a floating health spa for a California firm. She lay idle in a Bahamian backwater and was sold in 2001 to Middle Eastern scrappers. While under tow that summer en route to her demolition, she sank off the coast of South Africa. [Built by Chantiers de l'Atlantique, St.-Nazaire, France, 1964. 25,320 gross tons; 629 feet long; 82 feet wide. Steam turbines, twin screw. Service speed 20 knots. 1,090 passengers as built (72 first-class, 1,018 tourist-class).]

HAMBURG (1969) ~ Called the "Space Ship" during her American debut in the summer of 1969, the *Hamburg* is seen here (*above*) being launched on February 21, 1968. Originally intended for part-time transatlantic service, by the time she first sailed in March 1969, cruising was her full-time occupation. She made long, luxurious trips and was noted for her fine service and spaciousness, and for having television and radio in every cabin. The first new German liner to be built since 1939, she was never very successful. Costing some $24 million, impressive for that time, she was said to be the most spacious liner afloat. In 1973, however, soon after the struggling German-Atlantic Line sold off the *Hanseatic*, this ship was given that very popular name, but only for a few months. Soon, after little more than four years with German Atlantic, the ex-*Hamburg* was on the sales lists. Hapag-Lloyd planned to buy her as a replacement for its 1953 *Europa*, but the deal never materialized. Instead, she went to the Soviet Black Sea Steamship Company of Odessa, and was renamed *Maksim Gorky*. She started her new career on charter to a British film company, appearing as the fictional liner *Britannic* in the 1974 movie *Juggernaut*. Later she was chartered to the giant West German Neckermann Travel Company for worldwide cruising. The former German ship has been largely carrying Germans ever since. [Built by Deutsche Werft Shipyard, Hamburg, West Germany, 1969. 24,981 gross tons; 642 feet long; 90 feet wide. Steam turbines, twin screw. Service speed 23.5 knots. 790 cruise passengers.]

THE 1960s: A SHIFT IN TRADES / 97

After the *Hamburg* arrived at New York for the first time on June 26, 1969, she quickly set off on an introductory cruise with specially invited guests. A special publicity event was organized for the ship's return to port. The Sylvania Electric Company arranged for what it called the "Big Shot" by setting off 1,145 flashbulbs simultaneously aboard the ship at just after ten in the evening. The shot seen here (**above**) was taken from an office building at Battery Park in lower Manhattan. The ship was headed upriver when the shot was taken. An estimated 25,000 ship and camera buffs lined the Battery waterfront to witness the event.

The *Hamburg* was noted for her high standard of decor and decoration (**below**), and ranked as one of the most luxurious liners afloat in the late 1960s. However, within twenty years, in 1989, when the ship was used for a meeting between President Bush and President Gorbachev, reporters described the same interiors as "Soviet Deco."

VÖLKERFREUNDSCHAFT ∽ Swedish American Line's sturdy little *Stockholm*, used on the Atlantic run to New York, might have gone unnoticed if she had not collided with the *Andrea Doria* on July 25, 1956. The Italian Line flagship sank the next day; altogether there were 52 casualties. To some, the *Stockholm* was the villain. Repaired and returned to service, she was sold in late 1959 to the East German Government's Deutsche Seereederei, which refitted her as a trade union holiday cruise ship. She was renamed *Völkerfreundschaft* (**opposite, top**), which translates as "Peoples' (or International) Friendship." Mostly Communist Party members, workers and their families were rewarded with voyages on the Baltic, to the Black Sea, and occasionally to Cuba. Retired in 1985, she spent time laid up as the *Volker* and then did a stint (until 1989) as the *Fridtjof Nansen*, an accommodation ship at Oslo. She was sold to the Italian Star Lauro Cruises in 1989 and brought to Genoa, where she was to be rebuilt as the *Surriento*, then as the *Positano*. But that project never came to pass and instead she was rebuilt (despite her advanced age) for another Italian shipper, Nina Cruise Lines, which recommissioned her in the summer of 1994 as the thoroughly modernized *Italia Prima*. Flying the Italian colors, she cruised mostly in the Mediterranean. In 1999, she became the *Valtur Prima*, running seven-day charter cruises out of Montego Bay, Jamaica to Cuba and Mexico. [Built by Gotaverken Shipyard, Gothenburg, Sweden, 1948. 12,068 gross tons; 525 feet long; 69 feet wide. Gotaverken diesels, twin screw. Service speed 19 knots. 568 one-class passengers.]

98 / THE 1960S: A SHIFT IN TRADES

FRITZ HECKERT ~ The East German Deutsche Seerederei ran three other passenger ships in the 1960s: the specially-built *Fritz Heckert*; the 10,900-ton *Georg Büchner*, the former *Charlesville* of the Belgian Line; and the 11,900-ton *J. G. Fichte*, previously the French passenger ship *Claude Bernard*. The *Fritz Heckert* (**middle**) was East Germany's first experiment in actually building a new liner. She cruised to Norway and the Baltic in the summers, and to the Mediterranean and Black Seas in winter. Occasionally, she made longer trips to Cuba. She was a very comfortable ship, offering several public rooms, a 200-seat restaurant that could be made over as a cinema, and indoor and outdoor pools. All of her cabins were doubles. Her combination diesel-gas turbine engines were unique, but troublesome. By 1972, she was laid up at Stralsund and used as a moored accommodation ship. [Built by Mathias Thesen-Werft, Wismer, East Germany, 1961. 8,115 gross tons; 463 feet long; 58 feet wide. Diesel-gas turbine combination, twin screw. Service speed 18 knots. 377 cruise passengers.]

REGINA MARIS ~ For a time in the 1960s and 70s the *Regina Maris* (**bottom**) was one of West Germany's most popular cruise ships. Owned by the Lübeck Line, she cruised to Scandinavia, the British Isles, Spitzbergen, Iceland, the Canary Islands, the Mediterranean, and later further afield to Indonesia and Southeast Asia. But operations were increasingly troubled by high costs. Sold twice, in 1976 and 1979, the ship was considered for various uses — as a Caribbean gambling casino, as a Canadian cruise ship on the Great Lakes — but actually spent most of her time laid up. In 1983, she was sold to a Greek buyer, John S. Latsis, a tanker and construction billionaire. Renamed *Alexander*, she was extensively rebuilt at Hamburg and made over as an ultra-luxurious private yacht. The ship has been used only for pleasure cruises, serving the likes of former President Bush, Prince Charles, and members of the Saudi royal family, along with the Latsis family. She spends considerable time waiting, but is always fully staffed and provisioned. [Built by Lübecker Flenderwerke AG, Lübeck, West Germany, 1966. 5,813 gross tons; 390 feet long; 54 feet wide. Diesels, twin screw. Service speed 18 knots. 276 first-class passengers.]

CHAPTER SIX

The Modern Age of Cruising

On a warm summer's evening in July 2000, we sailed from Cuxhaven, the German port west of Hamburg, bound for a nostalgic cruise across the fabled North Atlantic. We sailed from the old Steubenhoft, a terminal used in bygone days by such famed ships as the *Albert Ballin*, the *Reliance*, the *Italia*, and the *Hanseatic*. Tens of thousands of passengers had passed through its halls and corridors before setting off across the seas. Framed, sepia-colored photos testified to the many ships that had berthed there. We sailed aboard the sumptuous 505-passenger *Deutschland*, owned by the German Peter Deilmann Cruises, easily one of the most splendidly decorated cruise ships afloat.

Thousands waved and cheered as the ship put to sea. "Germans are especially proud of the *Deutschland* and not only because she is very, very beautiful, but because she is German-built, German-owned and German-crewed. She is one of the very few totally ethnic cruise liners sailing today," noted a passenger from Düsseldorf. Furthermore, magazines and newspapers had been full of praise for her exceptional interior decor. "She is the most beautiful European cruise ship sailing today," noted a four-time repeat passenger.

The Atlantic crossing was full, mostly with Germans, many of whom wanted to feel something of those ocean passages of yesteryear. (One lecturer thoughtfully gave a series of talks on German emigration in steerage to Ellis Island, dubbed "Routes of the Roots.") The trip was, however, more cruise-like in tone, especially since we had no fewer than six port calls before reaching the shores of Manhattan. We put into Plymouth in England (for tours to lush Devon and enchanting Cornwall), Waterford in Ireland and then, in about four days, crossed to St. John's, Newfoundland; then to Charlottetown on Prince Edward Island; and finally Sydney and Halifax in Nova Scotia.

The 574-foot-long *Deutschland*, decorated by an architect who specializes in very grand hotels, is a magnificent vessel in every way. Peter Deilmann, the owner, took a deep personal interest in the project and, as an avid art collector, generously placed paintings and sculptures throughout the seven-deck ship. "She's absolutely reminiscent of a bygone era, probably the 1920s mostly," said a passenger from Bremen. "She's a blend of Edwardian and Art Nouveau. There are detailed ceilings, marble columns, brass handrails, rich woods, and ornate glass domes." She is indeed a proud member of the world's cruise fleet.

As I prepare this book in early 2001, the international cruise industry seems to be facing limitless growth. In the United States, cruising has become a $6 billion annual business. More people are traveling by ship than ever before and an average of two new ships a month are entering service. Even if over 90 percent of American vacationers have not yet taken a cruise, it is widely regarded as the best value of all vacation types, and the word is spreading. Almost always, the first cruise leads to the second, and then to more. It is "a glorious addiction," as one veteran cruiser told me.

The Holland America Line, now part of the mighty Carnival Group, is one of the major players in the US cruise market. With eleven passenger ships, it has the largest liner fleet in its 128-year history. Several 85,000-tonners now being built will be the largest Dutch liners ever. After some years under flags of convenience — the Dutch West Indies and the Bahamas — Holland America Line ships are back under Dutch colors.

European cruise travel is expanding rapidly as well, and the Germans in particular are experiencing considerable growth. Aida Cruises, now a part of London-based P&O, has ordered several new liners and added the 70,000-ton former *Crown Princess* to its fleet, for example. Hapag-Lloyd is running no fewer than four cruise ships, while Peter Deilmann is entering the riverboat markets on various European waterways, including those of France and Italy. The German market also supports a good number of charter cruise ships, such as the *Maksim Gorky*, the former *Hamburg*, and the *Albatros*, the onetime Cunard liner *Sylvania*. Germany is also one of the world's four leading builders of cruise ships, specifically at the extraordinary Meyer Werft plant in Papenburg. German ships are particularly known for their high quality.

So the history of Dutch and German passenger shipping, of companies like the Holland America Line and Hapag-Lloyd (Hamburg America and North German Lloyd), continues.

VEENDAM and VOLENDAM (1958) ~ By the early 1970s, as the age of Atlantic crossings all but ended, the Holland America Line became Holland America Cruises and began to offer full-time leisure voyages. Having sold the *Maasdam* and *Ryndam* (of 1951–52), and realizing that the *Nieuw Amsterdam* (of 1938), was nearing her end, the company needed to acquire new tonnage. But the idea of building new ships, especially larger ones just for cruises, seemed risky. Management considered a number of existing, out-of-work passenger vessels and decided on the sister ships *Argentina* and *Brasil*, built for the Moore McCormack Lines and noted for their high-quality construction. Laid up at Baltimore, these ships were rebuilt at Bremerhaven and reemerged as the *Veendam* **(above)** and *Volendam* in April and June of 1973. They concentrated on shorter cruises of seven to ten days; they had been intended to make long, expensive trips, such as 90-day around-the-world cruises, but proved fuel-hungry and quite costly from the start. During the fuel crisis of 1974–75, they were actually laid up for a time. For about a decade, they were great staples in the Holland America fleet. [Built by Ingalls Shipbuilding Corporation, Pascagoula, Mississippi, 1958. 23,395 gross tons; 617 feet long; 88 feet wide. Steam turbines, twin screw. Service speed 21 knots. 671 cruise passengers.]

When Holland America decided to build two new, larger liners, the *Nieuw Amsterdam* and *Noordam* of 1983–84, the pair of ex-American ships were made redundant. They were soon sold off, but have since gone through the greatest series of name changes in ocean liner history. The *Argentina*, which had become the *Veendam*, sailed briefly under charter (in 1974–75) as the *Brasil* and later the *Monarch Star*, reverted to *Veendam*, changed to *Bermuda Star*, *Enchanted Isle*, *Commodore Hotel*, and finally went back to *Enchanted Isle*. She cruised out of New Orleans to the Caribbean until 2000 and is now laid up. The original *Brasil*, which had become the *Volendam*, later became the *Monarch Sun*, reverted to *Volendam*, then became the *Island Sun*, *Liberté*, seen here in Tahitian waters in July 1986 **(below)**, *Canada Star*, *Queen of Bermuda*, *Enchanted Seas*, and finally *Universe Explorer*. She was running charter cruises by 2001—summers in Alaska and the remainder of the year on "floating university" trips around the world.

THE MODERN AGE OF CRUISING / 101

PRINSENDAM (1973) ~ In the early 1970s, Holland America planned a series of small, intimate cruise ships for unusual, smaller-port itineraries. Only one was actually built, the *Prinsendam*. At first, she ran year-round two-week cruises out of Singapore to the Indonesian islands, carrying mostly American and some European travelers on air-sea packages. Later, she was also assigned to the increasingly popular summertime service from Vancouver to Alaska. It was during a "positioning" cruise from Vancouver to the Far East in October 1980 that the *Prinsendam* prematurely met her end. She caught fire in the Gulf of Alaska and had to be abandoned (an extraordinary rescue effort by Canadian and American coast guards saved all passengers and crew). Days later, after all salvage attempts had failed, she was allowed to sink (*above*). [Built by De Merwede Shipyard, Hardinxveld, Netherlands, 1973. 8,566 gross tons; 427 feet long; 62 feet wide. Werkspor diesels, twin screw. Service speed 21 knots. 374 cruise passengers.]

EUROPA (1981) ~ "When the old passenger ship services were declining up to 1970, it became increasingly evident that cruising was the future," notes Arnold Kludas. "Hapag-Lloyd could have invested heavily like the Holland America Line, but they didn't. They missed the boat. With its long and very distinguished history in the passenger ship business, the Germans should have become a major player in the international cruise business. The Germans had strong cruising traditions from the 1930s. Americans had loved German ships, especially because the service was superior. The Germans had a strong hold, even despite Nazi government in the late 1930s. Instead, Hapag-Lloyd decided to concentrate on the very specific upper luxury market with the new *Europa* of 1981." Hapag-Lloyd had a huge following and a 70-percent repeat rate by 1980, and so decided to build one of the most luxurious liners of her time, under the legendary name *Europa*. The initial plan was to build her in two sections at two different shipyards, to appease different political factions. This never came to pass, however, and the ship was built entirely, and more practically, at Bremen. She cruised to ports around the world (*below*), on voyages from seven to 107 days long. But as cruise ship operations grew more competitive and efficient, she gradually fell out of step by the latter half of the 1990s. Yet another new *Europa* was added in the summer of 1999, and the 1981 ship was sold to the Malaysian-owned Star Cruises, for Asian cruising under the name *Super Star Europe*. [Built by Bremer-Vulkan Shipyard, Bremen, West Germany, 1981. 33,819 gross tons; 655 feet long; 92 feet wide. M.A.N. diesels, twin screw. Service speed 21 knots. 758 cruise passengers.]

The 1981 *Europa*'s splendid amenities included a bar-lounge (*opposite, top left*) and a sensibly partitioned restaurant (*opposite, top right*).

NOORDAM (1984) ~ In the early 1980s, Holland America built two of the finest cruise liners of their day, the sisters *Nieuw Amsterdam*, commissioned in June 1983, and *Noordam*, seen here at St.-Nazaire in April 1984 (*below*). Cleverly, it used contemporary decor highlighted by antiques, artifacts, and period fittings. The theme of the *Nieuw Amsterdam*'s collection was the Dutch West India Company, which had been responsible for the early settlement of Manhattan Island. Weapons, documents, vases, murals, statues, painted tiles, and even navigational instruments were included in the displays. The *Noordam* collection's theme was the Dutch East India Company and featured many Asian treasures. Initially, the two ships were used in summer service from Vancouver to Alaskan ports, and to the Caribbean for much of the remainder of the year. By the mid-1990s, they made more diverse cruises. The *Nieuw Amsterdam* was sold in the fall of 2000 to an American company under the revived name of United States Lines. Renamed *Patriot*, she cruised the Hawaiian Islands until being laid up in the fall of 2001. She is now sailing under charter in European waters as the *Thomson Spirit*. [Built by Chantiers de l'Atlantique, St.-Nazaire, France, 1984. 33,930 gross tons; 704 feet long; 90 feet wide. Sulzer diesels, twin screw. Service speed 21 knots. 1,210 cruise passengers.]

104 / THE MODERN AGE OF CRUISING

At various times since 1997, the Noordam (*opposite, top*) has been rumored to be for sale as well. Italy's Mediterranean Shipping Cruises and Britain's Saga Cruises are said to be interested. After her sister *Nieuw Amsterdam* left the company in the fall of 2000, the sixteen-year-old *Noordam* became the oldest member of Holland America's highly rated cruise service.

"A home away from home" is how Holland America describes a typical cabin on its ships. This room aboard the *Noordam*, for example, has individual temperature controls, telephone, radio, and multichannel television among its conveniences (*opposite, bottom*).

The main show rooms (*top*) on the *Nieuw Amsterdam* and *Noordam* were impressive in their day, but have long since been surpassed by theater-style rooms with over 1,500 seats. Staging now includes lighting, sound, and special effects that equal those of Broadway or Las Vegas.

WIND SPIRIT ∾ As the worldwide cruise industry expanded in the 1980s, new concepts were explored. One of these was the "sail cruise," which offered the "sail experience" in an otherwise conventionally powered vessel. The first to offer a sail cruise was Windstar Cruises' *Wind Star* in the fall of 1986; she was followed by two sisters, the *Wind Song* and the *Wind Spirit* (*bottom*). The sails, which are operated by computerized machinery and so use little manpower, are in operation during about half of each seven- or 14-day voyage. This "sailing" is done in daylight hours and only in tranquil waters. The format was an immediate success, especially among travelers wanting an unusual cruise experience. Other German companies operate more traditional sail-cruise ships, such as the *Sea Cloud I* and *Sea Cloud II*, and the smaller *Lili Marleen*. Windstar Cruises was sold in June 1987 to the Holland America Line, which was itself acquired the next year by Carnival Cruise Lines. [Built by Ateliers et Chantiers du Havre, Le Havre, France, 1986. 5,307 gross tons; 440 feet long; 52 feet wide. Diesels (auxiliary to sail power), twin screw. Service speed 12 knots maximum. 160 cruise passengers.]

THE MODERN AGE OF CRUISING / 105

WESTERDAM (1986) ~ Supported by its great profits, especially in the rapidly expanding US cruise market, Holland America bought Windstar in June 1987 and the acclaimed, long-established Home Lines in April 1988. From that combination Italian-Greek-Swiss company, it inherited two cruise liners, the 30,200-ton *Atlantic* and the very new 42,000-ton *Homeric*. Transfers were made that fall, just as Holland America itself was bought by Carnival (for $625 million). The *Atlantic* was resold immediately to Florida's Premier Cruise Lines to become the *Starship Atlantic*, sailing on three- and four-day cruises to the Bahamas. The *Homeric* remained with Holland America as the *Westerdam*. It was soon decided, however, that she needed to be larger, for greater profitability. She was returned to her West German builders at Papenburg, cut in half, and had a new, 130-foot midsection added. Her tonnage increased to 53,872, her length from 670 to 798 feet and her passenger capacity from 1,030 to 1,476. She returned to New York on March 21, 1990 *(top)* as virtually a different ship. It was the largest "stretching" of a liner yet undertaken. [Built by Meyer Werft, Papenburg, West Germany, 1986. 53,872 gross tons as lengthened; 798 feet long; 95 feet wide. Burmeister & Wain diesels, twin screw. Service speed 22.5 knots. 1,476 cruise passengers.]

MAASDAM (1993) ~ Just after Carnival acquired Holland America Line in November 1988, plans were set in motion for new ships, improved versions of the *Nieuw Amsterdam* and *Noordam*, slightly larger than the rebuilt *Westerdam*. Originally, three ships were planned, dubbed the "S Class," the *Statendam*, *Stellendam*, and *Schiedam*, but in the event, four ships were built, named *Statendam*, *Maasdam*—seen here outbound from Lisbon *(bottom)*—*Ryndam*, and *Veendam*. The *Statendam* was given a particularly rousing reception when she arrived at Port Everglades on her maiden voyage from Italy in January 1993. The *Maasdam* followed that November. [Built by Fincantieri, Monfalcone, Italy, 1993. 55,400 gross tons; 720 feet long; 90 feet wide. Diesels, twin screw. Service speed 20 knots. 1,600 cruise passengers.]

106 / THE MODERN AGE OF CRUISING

Holland America has changed its funnel colors on at least two occasions since the early 1970s. The latest change involves the use of the company logo, which depicts *Nieuw Amsterdam* of 1938 behind Henry Hudson's little *Half Moon*, a graphic allusion to the long history of Dutch seafaring. The *Maasdam*, seen here at Lisbon on April 28, 1996 *(left)*, called at Rotterdam in August 1995, the first Holland America liner to do so in over twenty years. A year later, in May 1996, she transferred to the Dutch flag, like almost all the Holland America liners, which had been sailing under Bahamian and Dutch West Indian flags of convenience. Home ports were changed to Rotterdam as well.

The *Maasdam* and her sisters are known as luxurious but understated ships. Again, antiques and period artifacts are incorporated into a contemporary decor. Public areas include a large lido restaurant, a 745-seat, two-level main restaurant *(below)* with a Murano glass ceiling, a three-deck-high atrium/lobby, a 600-seat, two-deck-high theater, and a midships lido area with a retractable glass roof. The ship's 631 cabins include 28 master suites with private verandahs and dining areas.

THE MODERN AGE OF CRUISING / 107

108 / THE MODERN AGE OF CRUISING

BERLIN (1980) ⟿ Its experience from 1979 to 1983 with the earlier *Regina Maris* convinced Germany's Peter Deilmann Company that there was a future for a better, slightly larger version of that ship. The *Berlin*, built in 1980, was designed to accommodate exactly one jumbo jetload of passengers (convenient for air-sea cruises), with a few spaces left over for relief staff. Aimed at the German market, she was chartered out in 1984, however, to run two-week cruises from Singapore as the *Princess Mahsuri* for a short-lived firm called Blue Funnel Cruises. She was back in Deilmann's service within months and, by 1986, had grown so popular that she was "stretched" by 90 feet to increase her capacity. Her popularity led Deilmann to build the larger, more lavish *Deutschland* in 1998. The *Berlin* is seen here *(opposite, top)* at Valletta, Malta in this view dated October 1987. [Built by HDW Shipyard, Kiel, West Germany, 1980. 9,570 gross tons as rebuilt; 457 feet long; 57 feet wide. Diesels, twin screw. Service speed 18 knots. 468 cruise passengers.]

ASTOR (1981) ⟿ Supported by the growth of the European cruise market, especially in prosperous West Germany, the Hadag Company, a Hamburg firm known for its small excursion vessels, decided to enter the deep-sea liner trade. Specifically, it wanted to compete directly with Hapag-Lloyd in the upper end of the German market. It planned a luxuriously comfortable ship with a capacity for about 600 passengers. Although Hadag at first had intended to call her *Hammonia*, she was christened the *Astor*, a reminder of the famed Astor family. She was a very German ship in almost all ways, but largely unsuccessful. Hapag-Lloyd, which had just added its brand-new, ultraluxurious *Europa*, remained secure in the top position of the West German luxury cruise trade. The *Astor* was sold in 1984 to the Capetown-based South African Marine Corporation (operating as Safmarine Lines), for cruising as well as a revival of the Capetown-Southampton liner service that had been run by the Union Castle Line until 1977. In this she was also unsuccessful. Her South African registry was also a liability in the international market. In the summer of 1985, she was sold to Deutsche Seerederei, a company owned by the East German government, which at first planned to rename her *Our Happy Country* for workers' cruises, but decided instead to concentrate on the lucrative West German charter market and rechristened her the *Arkona (opposite, bottom)*, a reminder of the legendary *Cap Arcona* of the 1920s and 30s. She has continued in European cruise service ever since for the tour operator Deutsche Seetouristic, postcommunist successor to the former East German company. She is seen departing from Copenhagen on June 4, 1993. [Built by HDW Shipyard, Hamburg, West Germany, 1981. 18,835 gross tons; 535 feet long; 73 feet wide. M.A.N. diesels, twin screw. Service speed 18 knots. 638 cruise passengers.]

ASTOR (1987) ⟿ Despite its failure with the *Astor*, South Africa's Safmarine Lines remained hopeful for its future in cruising. In 1985, it ordered a slightly larger, slightly different version of the previous *Astor*. This ship too was named *Astor*, but registered in politically less-sensitive Mauritius, staffed by Mauritians and operated by a British-based firm called Morgan Leisure (Astor Cruises). But this *Astor* too was highly unsuccessful. She could not quite find a place in the upper end of the British and European cruise market and within a year was sold to the Soviet Odessa-based Black Sea Steamship Company. She was named *Feodor Dostoevsky*, shown here together with the *Maksim Gorky* at Lisbon on December 26, 1990 *(above)*, and was used primarily for charter cruises with Western passengers, mostly Germans. In 1995, she was sold to Russian-German cooperative owners, renamed *Astor* and chartered to Transmarin, a German tour operator. [Built by HDW Shipyard, Hamburg, West Germany, 1987. 20,159 gross tons; 578 feet long; 74 feet wide. Sulzer diesels, twin screw. Service speed 18 knots. 650 cruise passengers.]

THE MODERN AGE OF CRUISING / 109

110 / THE MODERN AGE OF CRUISING

AIDA ~ The German tour operator Deutsche Seetouristik (the former East German Deutsche Seerederei) decided shortly after German reunification to build a new liner for the growing German mass-market cruise business of the 1990s. The colorfully-painted *Aida* has been operated mainly on charters and for a time was owned by Miami-based Norwegian Cruise Lines and leased back to Deutsche Seetouristik, which then did business as Aida Cruises. The ship was resold to the German company, which itself was then sold to the British P&O Company. By 2000, Aida Cruises was constructing several new liners as well as operating the *Arkona* and P&O's 70,000-ton *Crown Princess*. By 2000, the German cruise market had grown to over 300,000 passengers (the far larger US market has 4 million and the British 700,000). The *Aida* is seen here (*opposite, top*) during her maiden cruise, arriving at Lisbon on June 16, 1996. [Built by Kvaener Masa Yards, Turku, Finland. 38,531 gross tons; 634 feet long; 90 feet wide. Diesels, twin screw. Service speed 21 knots. 1,186 cruise passengers.]

BREMEN (1990) ~ The *Bremen* (*opposite, bottom*) is run by Hapag-Lloyd for the adventure cruise market. Itineraries include the Amazon River, Cape Horn, Antarctica, the Seychelles, the Scottish isles, Greenland, and Iceland. Originally named *Frontier Spirit*, she was built for a cooperative company called Frontier Cruises, whose partners included Hapag-Lloyd and the Japanese firms Nippon Yusen Kaisha and the NYK Line, parent of Crystal Cruises. In 1993, Hapag-Lloyd took over the ship completely and renamed her *Bremen*. Currently, she sails under the Bahamian flag. She has six passenger decks that include eighteen cabins with private verandahs, an observation lounge, library, conference room, sauna and gym, outdoor pool, and single-seating restaurant. Her 15-foot draft allows for visits to very remote small ports, and she carries Zodiac landing craft for spontaneous visits ashore. Her onboard entertainment usually includes expert lecturers on topics such as geography, history, and flora and fauna. By 1996, published fares were approximately $600 per person per day for a standard outside cabin and $1,100 per person per day for a suite with verandah. [Built by Mitsubishi Heavy Industries, Kobe, Japan, 1990. 6,752 gross tons; 365 feet long; 55 feet wide. Diesels, twin screw. Service speed 17 knots. 184 cruise passengers.]

HANSEATIC (1991) ~ Hapag-Lloyd is not the only shipping line—with the *Europa*, the *Bremen*, and the *Columbus*—to reuse for its cruise ships the names of great liners of the past. The German-owned, Bahamian-registered Hanseatic Tours has done the same. The *Society Adventurer* was built for German owners, who intended her for a long-term charter to Seattle-based Society Expeditions. Financial problems, however, caused the incomplete ship to sit idle for a time before being bought by Hanseatic. Renamed *Hanseatic*, she was soon placed in operation with the Hapag-Lloyd cruise ships. She too follows the adventure cruise pattern, traveling to remote ports in places such as Canada, Alaska, Siberia, and Japan. She has also made trips to Antarctica. Among her amenities is a large observation lounge and a 170-seat lecture hall. She is seen here (*below*) berthed at Sitka, Alaska in July 1996. [Built by Rauma Yards, Rauma, Finland, 1991. 8,378 gross tons; 402 feet long; 59 feet wide. Diesels, twin screw. Service speed 16 knots. 188 cruise passengers.]

THE MODERN AGE OF CRUISING / 111

DEUTSCHLAND (1998) ~ The Peter Deilmann Company, with considerable interests in the expanding European river cruise business, ventured into the high end of the European market with the creation of the *Deutschland (above)*. Her art- and antique-filled interiors evoke the Edwardian era of ocean travel and include such details as polished dark woods, crystal chandeliers, and stained glass skylights. She follows the pattern set by Hapag-Lloyd's *Europa*, roaming the globe on constantly varied itineraries. In the summer of 2000, for example, she made a 60-day cruise that took her from Hamburg to Sydney, where she was used as a hotel for the Olympics. That voyage included calls at the Canadian Maritimes, New York, Florida, the Panama Canal, Ecuador, Easter Island, and Tahiti. The *Deutschland* is impeccably furnished and flawlessly served to suit her demanding, well-traveled guests; one passenger has said that dining on her is "like eating in the best Berlin restaurant every night." [Built by HDW Shipyard, Kiel, Germany, 1998. 21,903 gross tons; 546 feet long; 78 feet wide. Diesels, twin screw. Service speed 18 knots. 607 cruise passengers.]

EUROPA (1999) ~ Hapag-Lloyd's *Europa*, commissioned in the summer of 1999, is considered the finest cruise ship in German service. Like her predecessors, she has exceptional decor and fine service for her wealthy passengers. Like her predecessors, she caters for a "millionaire set," passengers who come year after year, on voyage after voyage, making her something of a floating club. Her amenities include indoor and outdoor pools, an Asian grill room, a conference and computer center, luxury suites that include walk-in saunas, and this spectacular seven-deck-high atrium, with piano bar, glass elevators and wood paneling *(opposite, top)*. She is the first cruise ship anywhere to include a computer in every cabin. She travels on changing itineraries; her maiden season included a world cruise that lasted five and a half months. Seen here at Valletta, Malta on October 1999 *(opposite, bottom)*, she continues the fine traditions of the great German liners and in particular those of two of the world's most historic shipping companies, the Hamburg America Line and North German Lloyd. [Built by Kvaerner Masa Yards, Helsinki, Finland, 1999. 28,400 gross tons; 650 feet long; 79 feet wide. Diesels, twin screw. Service speed 19 knots. 408 cruise passengers.]

THE MODERN AGE OF CRUISING / 113

REMBRANDT ~ On October 28, 1998, Premier Cruise Lines' *Rembrandt*, the former Holland America flagship *Rotterdam*, perhaps the most beloved of the latter-day Dutch liners, made her first return to Rotterdam in nearly thirty years *(above)*. Her visit was a reminder of earlier days of ocean liner travel: of class-divided transocean sailings, of "ships of state," of distinctive national styles of liner operations.

ROTTERDAM (1997) ~ In the wake of the great success of the ships of the 55,000-ton *Statendam* class, Holland America has embarked on the greatest passenger shipbuilding program in its history. A new flagship was the order of business in 1996. She would be the largest, most luxurious and fastest liner in the company's history. Known informally as the "Fastdam," she was named *Rotterdam*, replacing the veteran flagship of 1959 which was being retired and sold in 1997. The new ship arrived shortly thereafter to great praise, and to further orders for as many as six more liners. A near-sister, the *Amsterdam*, arrived in the fall of 2000 and has been proclaimed the line's "second flagship." Other new ships include the *Volendam* and *Zaandam*. Holland America celebrated its great heights of popularity and profitability on the occasion of the company's 125th anniversary in 1998. Official banquets, luncheons, and tours were conducted at Rotterdam, and there was a gala fireworks display *(below)* during the *Rotterdam*'s first visit to her namesake port in June. [Built by Fincantieri Shipyard, Marghera, Italy, 1997. 59,652 gross tons; 767 feet long; 102 feet wide. Diesels, twin screw. Service speed 25 knots. 1,668 cruise passengers.]

Bibliography

BOOKS

Bonsor, N. R. P. *North Atlantic Seaway.* Prescot, Lancashire: T. Stephenson & Sons Limited, 1955.

—— *South Atlantic Seaway.* Channel Islands: Brookside Publications, 1983.

Braynard, Frank O. *Lives of the Liners.* New York: Cornell Maritime Press, 1947.

Braynard, Frank O. and William H. Miller. *Fifty Famous Liners*, Volumes 1–3. Cambridge: Patrick Stephens Ltd., 1982–86.

Cooper, James and Duncan Haws. *Merchant Ships: Rotterdam Lloyd.* Uckfield, England: T. C. L. Publications, 1998.

De Groot, Edward P. *Per Mailboot naar Amerika.* Bussum, Netherlands: Uniebok BV, 1980.

Dunn, Laurence. *Passenger Liners.* Southampton: Adlard Coles Limited, 1961.

—— *Passenger Liners*, Revised Edition. Southampton: Adlard Coles Ltd., 1965.

Durand, Jean-Francois. *Cruise Ships Around the World.* Nantes, France: Marines Edition, 1997.

Haws, Duncan. *Merchant Ships: Holland America Line.* Uckfield, England: T. C. L. Publications, 1995.

Kludas, Arnold. *Die Geschichte der deutschen Passagierschiffahrt,* Volumes 1–5. Hamburg: Ernst Kabel Verlag, 1990.

—— *Great Passenger Ships of the World,* Volumes 1–5. Cambridge, England: Patrick Stephens Ltd., 1972–76.

—— *Great Passenger Ships of the World,* Volume 6. Cambridge: Patrick Stephens Ltd., 1986.

—— *Great Passenger Ships of the World Today.* Sparkford, England: Patrick Stephens Ltd., 1992.

—— *Die grossen Passagier-Schiffe der Welt.* Hamburg: Koehlers Verlagsgesellschaft mbH, 1997.

—— *Die Schnelldampfer Bremen und Europa.* Herford, Germany: Koehlers Verlagsgesellschaft, 1993.

—— *The Ships of the German-Africa Line.* Oldenburg: Verlag Gerhard Stalling AG, 1975.

—— *The Ships of the Hamburg-Sud 1871–1951.* Oldenburg: Verlag Gerhard Stalling AG, 1976.

Le Fleming, H. M. *Ships of the Holland America Line.* London: John Marshbank Ltd., 1963.

Miller, William H. *The Cruise Ships.* London: Conway Maritime Press Ltd., 1988.

—— *German Ocean Liners of the 20th Century.* Wellingborough, Northamptonshire: Patrick Stephens Ltd., 1989.

—— *The Great Luxury Liners 1927–1954.* New York: Dover Publications, Inc., 1981.

—— *The Last Atlantic Liners.* London: Conway Maritime Press Ltd., 1985.

—— *The Last Blue Water Liners.* London: Conway Maritime Press Ltd., 1986.

—— *Pictorial Encyclopedia of Ocean Liners, 1860–1994.* Mineola, New York: Dover Publications, Inc., 1995.

—— *Transatlantic Liners 1945–80.* Newton Abbot, Devon: David & Charles Ltd., 1981.

Praeger, Hans Georg. *Blohm & Voss: Ships and Machinery for the World.* Herford: Koehlers Verlagsgesellschaft, 1977.

Schaap, Dick. *A Bridge to the Seven Seas.* New York: Holland America Cruises, 1973.

Schmidt, Robert and Arnold Kludas. *Die Deutschen Lazarettschiffe in Zweiten Weltkrieg.* Stuttgart: Motorbuch Verlag, 1978.

Smith, Eugene W. *Passenger Ships of the World Past and Present.* Boston: George H. Dean Company, 1963.

Van Herk, Cornelius. *The Ships of the Holland America Line.* Haarlem: Historiche Boekhandel Erato, 1981.

Witthoft, Hans Jurgen. *Hapag-Lloyd.* Herford: Koehlers Verlagsgesellschaft, 1979.

PERIODICALS

Cruise Travel. Evanston, Illinois: World Publishing Company, 1996–2000.

Marine News (Michael Crowdy, ed.). Kendal, Cumbria: World Ship Society, 1964–2000.

Ocean and Cruise News (George Devol, ed.). Stamford, Connecticut: World Ocean & Cruise Society, 1980–2000.

Ships Monthly. Burton-on-Trent, England: Country & Leisure Media Ltd., 1990–2000.

Steamboat Bill (Peter Eisele and William Rau, eds.). New York: Steamship Historical Society of America, Inc., 1964–2000.

Index of Ships

Page numbers in **boldface** type indicate entry headings. Page numbers in *italic* refer to illustrations.
To distinguish between ships that have the same names, dates are given in parentheses.
The date shown is the year a ship began sailing under that name (*not* the year the ship was first launched).

Achille Lauro 68
Admiral Nakhimov 20
Admiral von Tirpitz 4
Adolph Woermann **45**, *45*
Aida 110, **111**
Albatros 100
Albert Ballin 1, **2**, 3, 4, 57, 100
Albiero 68
Aldabi 68
Alexander 99
Alhena 68
Alnati **68**, 69
America 70
American Scout 82, *82*
Amerika 2
Amsterdam 115
Andrea Doria 98
Angelina Lauro 62
Ardjoeno 66
Arendsdijk 52, 53
Argentina 101
Ariadne **86**, *86*
Ariane 86
Arkona 108, 109, 111
Arosa Sun **81**, *81*
Astor (1981) **109**
Astor (1987) 109
Athenia 63
Atlantic 106
Atlas 72
Avare 57

Baloeran ix, 38, **39**, 63
Banfora 33
Banfora Maru 33
Batoer 66
Bayernstein **85**, *85*
Berengaria ix, 2
Bergensfjord 22
Berlin (1925) **20**, *21*, 54
Berlin (1955) 70, **82**, *83*, 88
Berlin (1980) 108, **109**
Bermuda Star 101
Bismarck ix, 2
Blijdendijk 52, 53
Blitar 68
Boissevain 61
Bon Vivant 86
Bonaire Star 62
Brabantia 4
Brasil 101
Bremen (1929) ix, 1, 8, 22, **23**, *23*, 24, 25, 26, 28, 29, *29*, *30–31*, *30*, 57, 63, 70

Bremen (1959) ix, 82, **88**, *89*
Bremen (1993) **111**, *110*
Britannic 85
Britannic (fictional) 97

Canada Star 101
Canberra 95
Cap Arcona ix, 1, 15, *15*, **17**, *17*, *18*, *19*, 63, 109
Cap Polonio **15**
Caribia 39
Caronia 50
Charlesville 99
Christiaan Huygens 34, **35**
Cincinnati 7
Claude Bernard 99
Cleveland 6, 7
Colombia 38, **39**
Columbus (1914) ix, 7
Columbus (1924) 1, 6, **7**, *7*, 8, *8*, 23, 25, *25*
Columbus (1997) 111
Columbus "C" 96
Commodore Hotel 101
Constitution 70, 82, *82*
Cordillera **39**, *39*
Costa Rica Victory 68
Cranston Victory 68
Crown Princess 100, 111

Delftdyk 63
Dempo ix, 38, **39**, 63
Der Deutsche 54
Deutschland (1900) 2, 4
Deutschland (1998) ix, 70, 100, 109, **112**, *112*
Diemerdyk **77**, *77*, 79
Diemerdyk (proposed) 71, 77
Dinteldyk **77**, 79
Dinteldyk (proposed) 71, 77
Dongedyk **78**, *79*
Doric 93, 96
Dresden 48, **49**

Edam **12**, *12*
Empire Doon 44
Empire Fowey 42
Empire Jewel 42
Empire Orwell 44
Empire Tarne 57
Empire Waveney 64, 65
Empire Welland 47
Empress Katerina 86
Empress of Australia 4

Empress of Britain 63
Empress of Japan 88
Empress of Scotland 70, 88
Enchanted Isle 101
Enchanted Seas 101
Europa (1930) ix, 1, 4, 8, 22, **23**, *23*, 24, 25, 26, *26*, 27, *27*, 28, 29, *29*, 30, *30*, 32, 57
Europa (1965) **96**, *96*, 97
Europa (1981) vii, 96, **102**, *102*, 103, 109, 111
Europa (1999) 102, 111, **112**, *113*

Felix Roussel 81
Feodor Dostoevsky 109, *109*
Filipinas Saudi I 88
Frankfurt **84**, **85**, *85*
Freeport II 86
Fridtjof Nansen 98
Fritz Heckert **99**, *99*

Garoet 68
General G. M. Randall 22
General von Steuben 20
Georg Büchner 99
George Washington ix, 2
Gneisenau **41**, *42*, 42
Gripsholm (1925) **82**
Gripsholm (1957) 82, *82*
Groote Beer 68
Grussgott 1
Gunung Djati 44

Hamburg (1926) 2, **4**, *4*, 29, *29*
Hamburg (1954) 85
Hamburg (1969) 96, **97**, *97*, 98, *98*, 100
Hammonia 109
Hannover 85
Hansa (1920) **2**, *2*
Hansa (1935) **2**, *3*
Hanseatic (1958) 70, **88**, *88*, 96, 100
Hanseatic (1966) **96**, *96*, 97
Hanseatic (1991) **111**, *111*
Hessenstein 85
Hindenburg 7
HMS Hyperion 8
Homeland 82
Homeric (1922) ix, 7
Homeric (1955) 82, *82*
Homeric (1986) 106

Iberia 47
Imperator ix, 2, 4
Independence 70
Insulinde **33**, *33*
Island Sun 101
Italia **82**, *83*, 100
Italia Prima 98

J. G. Fichte 99
Jerusalem 62
Johan van Oldenbarnevelt ix, **35**, *35*, 36, *36*, 37, 39, 70
Johann Heinrich Burchard 4
Josif Stalin 65
Justicia 12

Karlsruhe **25**, *25*
Kazakhstan 93
King Alexander 7
Kota Makmur 68
Kungsholm 82, 96

La Grande Victory 68
Lakonia 36
Lancastria 63
Langkoeas 68
Leerdam (1921) 12, 52, 53
Leviathan ix, 2
Liberté (1950) 32, *32*, 82, *82*
Liberté (1986) **101**, *101*
Lili Marleen 105
Limburgia 4
Lombardia 4

Maasdam (1921) 12
Maasdam (1952) ix, 70, **71**, *71*, 72, *72*, 73, 74, 77, 91, 95, 101
Maasdam (1983) 107
Maasdam (1993) 70, **106**, *106*, 107
Magdalena 46, **47**
Majestic ix, 2
Maksim Gorky 97, 100, 109, *109*
Marnix van St Aldegonde 35, 39, 63
Mataram 68
Mauretania ix, 23, 25, 82, *82*
Michelangelo 96
Milwaukee **19**, *19*, 20, *20*, 65
Monarch Star 101
Monarch Sun 101
Monte Cervantes 16, 17
Monte Olivia 17

Monte Pascoal 17
Monte Rosa 16, **17**
Monte Sarmiento 17
Mormacmail 85
München **20**, 21, 47, *47*

Nelly 85
Neptunia 57
New York 4, **65**, *65*
Nieuw Amsterdam (1906) 10
Nieuw Amsterdam (1938) ix, 15, **49**, *49*, 50, *50*, 51, 52, *52*, 53, 54, *54*, 55, 59, 61, 74, 91, 95, 101, 107
Nieuw Amsterdam (1983) 101, 103, *105*, 105, 106
Nieuw Holland 34, **35**
Nieuw Zeeland 35
Noordam (1938) 52, 53, 58, **59**
Noordam (1984) 101, **103**, *103*, 104, 105, 106
Normandie 26, 30, 63

Ocean Monarch 82, *82*
Oceana 56, **57**
Oceanic 93
Oceanien 59
Oranje ix, **61**, *61*, 62, *62*, 66
Oranje Nassau 70, 80, **81**
Ormuz 49
Oslofjord 63
Our Happy Country 109

Pasteur 88
Patria ix, **32**, 33, *33*, 41, 47
Patricia 86
Patriot 103
Peer Gynt 57
Pennland 61
Positano 98
Potsdam 41
Pretoria **44**, *44*
Princess Mahsuri 109
Prins der Nederlanden 81
Prins Willem van Oranje 81
Prinsendam **102**, *102*

Prinsendam (proposed) 49
Prinses Irene 80, **81**
Prinses Margriet 81

Queen Elizabeth 70
Queen Elizabeth 2 93
Queen Mary 26, 70
Queen of Bermuda 101

Randfontein 70, **79**, *79*
Regent Star 76
Regent Sun 96
Regina Magna 88
Regina Maris **99**, *99*, 109
Reliance 1, 4, 5, **29**, *29*, 48, **49**, 100
Rembrandt 94, *114*, 114
Resolute 4
Rex 26, 30, 63
Rhapsody 76
Robert Ley 56, **57**, *64*, 65
Rossia 46, *47*
Rotterdam (1908) **10**, *10*, 11
Rotterdam (1959) *ii–iii*, ix, 70, 74, 90–91, **91**, 92, 93, *93*, 94, *94*, 95, 114
Rotterdam (1997) **115**, *115*
Royal Odyssey 96
Ruys 60, **61**
Ryndam (1951) ix, 71, 72, 74, 77, 91, 101
Ryndam (1994) 106

Safina-e-Hujjaj 42
Santa Catarina 86
Santa Elena 86, 87
Santa Ines 86
Santa Isabel **86**, 87
Santa Teresa 86
Santa Ursula 86
Santos Maru 44
Sarah Bowater 82, *82*
Saturnia 82, *82*
Saudi Phil I 88
Scharnhorst 40–41, **41**, *42*, 43
Schiedam 106

Schwaben 8
Schwabenstein 85
Sea Cloud I 105
Sea Cloud II 105
Seven Seas 70, 84, **85**
Shinyo 42
Sibajak **33**, *33*
Sibir 57
Sierra Salvada 57
Slamat 68, 69
Society Adventurer 111
Sovetsky Sojus 2
Soyuz 2
Spaarndam 12
St. Louis 19, 20
Starship Atlantic 106
Statendam (1914) 12
Statendam (1929) ix, 1, **12**, *13*, 14, 63
Statendam (1957) 70, 71, **74**, *74*, 75, 76, *76*, 91, 93, 95
Statendam (1992) 106, 115
Stavangerfjord 22
Stefan Batory 70, 72, 73
Stellendam 106
Steuben 20, 63
Stockholm 98
Strassburg 39
Stuttgart 54
Super Star Europe 102
Surriento 98
Svir 32
Sylvania 100

Tanjung Pandan 44
Tegelberg 61
Tirpitz ix, 4
Tjiluwah 79
Tjiwangi ix, 78, **79**

United States 70
Universe Explorer 101
Usaramo 44, **45**
USS Europa 32
USS John Ericsson 82
USS Lejeune 44

USS Leviathan 2
USS Long Island 85
USS Mobile 7
USS Tuscaloosa 8

Valtur Prima 98
Vaterland (1914) ix, 2
Vaterland (1940) **57**, *57*
Veendam (1923) 9
Veendam (1973) **101**, *101*
Veendam (1996) 106
Victoria 22
Victoria Luise 2
Viktoria 57
Vineta 15
Vistafjord vii
Volendam (1922) **9**, *9*
Volendam (1973) **101**
Volendam (1999) 115
Volker 98
Völkerfreundschaft **98**, *98*, 99
Voltaire 44, 45

Waterman 68, 69
Westerdam (1946), **59**, *59*, 95
Westerdam (1986) **106**, *106*
Westernland 60, **61**
Wilhelm Gustloff **54**, 55, 56, 57, 63
Willem Ruys ix, 62, **66**, *66*, 67, 68, *68*
William O'Swald 4
Wind Song 105
Wind Spirit **105**, *105*
Wind Star 105
Windhuk 44
Wuri 68

Yuri Dolgoruki 4

Zaandam (1939) 59
Zaandam (2000) 115
Zeppelin 49
Zuiderdam 59
Zuiderkruis 68